MW00329615

The Fascinating Girl Vintage Edition
By Helen B. Andelin
Edited and Revised by Dixie Andelin Forsyth
Cover Art by Shintayu Arifin
Interior Design by Richard A. Forsyth

ISBN: 978-1-946032-06-5

For information, write:

Fascinating Womanhood
Box 3831
Springfield, Missouri 65809
Published by
Axicon Circle, LLC

Dedicated to every girl in the world.
Each one I revere as a potential Fascinating Woman.

There is in this world no function more important than that of being charming—to shed joy around—to cast light upon dark days. Is not this to render a service?

~ Victor Hugo

The Fascinating Girl

Vintage Edition

Table of Contents

Editor's Forward

This book was originally published in 1969. Before my mother passed away, we talked about the need to update parts of it. Over forty-five years ago, the dating and cultural landscape was quite different. I have approached editing of this vintage edition with the desire to maintain the original enduring principles while removing the most dated and non-essential aspects of it. I have left some of the charming but dated ways of saying things you'll notice throughout.

In addition, I am aware that some might look on various "strategies" with men as manipulative. The dilemma women have faced throughout time has been how to attract a man they love without being too aggressive—a trait seldom, if ever, appreciated by men. We have always used femininity and charm to successfully do our part to get a man's attention. We must use what advantages we have. In any case, the essence of manipulation is selfishness. Good women, who are in love, are interested in not just what they want, but what the man they love wants too. This approach is winning with men. It leads to their happiness as well as ours. That is what makes it not manipulative but influential in a positive, feminine way.

You may notice Christian scripture references have been omitted from the original. This is so that our worldwide audience can focus on the essence of dating and preparing for lifelong romantic marriages without referencing any particular religious perspective. I have had a number of women ask me if the principles of Fascinating Womanhood apply to those who are not Christian. The answer of course is yes. A true principle will hold up no matter what specific religious authority is referenced to support it.

I hope you enjoy this vintage edition of The Fascinating Girl. It still has a profound message and insights into understanding men and a glimpse into the vast power of femininity.

I am sensitive to young women who want the companionship of a lifelong love. There are many things you can do that will empower you in relationships and as a woman.

On a personal note, as I was editing this book, I couldn't help but hear my mother's voice teaching me these principles when I was very young. She first began writing when I was only about 9, before I even liked boys. She wrote like she spoke. It brought back many emotions and memories. I appreciate the opportunity to carry on some of her legacy.

This book is a foundational companion, along with Fascinating Womanhood, to my new book which combines both books titled "Fascinating Womanhood for the Timeless Woman". Together, these books blend traditional wisdom with the next generation of essential ideas and perspectives that will elevate you to the highest levels of relationship development. You are invited to read on and learn the precious secrets fascinating women have guarded throughout the ages that are now being revealed again.

A Word of Explanation by the Author

Part I of this book is based upon the teachings of a former book I have written to married women, entitled Fascinating Womanhood. Where teachings parallel it has been necessary, for principles in winning men are essentially the same as for keeping them and making them happy. This book has its special approach, however, and much additional information has been added specifically for the single girl.

It is a wholesome book written as a guide for girls approaching the marriageable age and is intended to offset some of the false and immoral teachings of our day. Many of the teachings of this book were inspired by a series of booklets published in the 1920s, entitled Fascinating Womanhood. These booklets have long been out of print and the authors unknown. Part II of this present work, "Strategy With Men," has been freely adapted from these booklets.

The Secrets of Fascinating Womanhood

We have all known women who have that "certain charm" which attracts men. Men flock around them like bees to honey, competing with one another for attention. These adorables seem to cast a spell upon almost any man they meet, while other girls who seem just as admirable and attractive go unnoticed and unappreciated.

What is this magical element of charm that wins the attention of men? Is it a pretty face? Not necessarily. Natural beauty is an advantage, but it is not essential. Many girls who possess only slight physical beauty are fascinating to men, while others, who are strikingly beautiful, from an artistic viewpoint, fail to interest many men. Is it good grooming? Attractive clothes?

To some extent it is, for a careless girl is not appealing to men. But there are girls who dress in the most stylish fashions and who are meticulous in their appearance who still fail to win a man's attention.

It is not necessarily wit, talent or intellectual gifts. These qualities are an advantage to any girl, but they are not the elements of real feminine charm.

No, there are girls who possess all these qualities; they are beautiful, well groomed, becomingly dressed, and in addition are witty, intelligent and talented, yet they fail to win men's hearts. Other girls have none of these virtues to any great degree and yet captivate and fascinate men.

The girl who has this "special charm," who succeeds in winning the attention of a wide circle of men friends, unfortunately does not always win the man of her choice. This was the situation with Scarlett O'Hara in the novel Gone with the Wind. Scarlett was sought after by almost every young man in the community, but the man she thought she really wanted, she could not win. There was something missing in her, from this young man's viewpoint; something he thought essential to his happiness and something which he found flowing freely in someone else — Melanie. To be prepared, therefore, for the time when the right young man comes along, the one you really want, it is important that you acquire all the elements of feminine charm.

This book is devoted to a study of these essentials and will explain to you the principles involved in not only winning the attention and interest of many men, but in awakening the deepest feelings of love and tenderness in a good man.

Is Sex One of the Secrets of Winning Men?

There is a mistaken idea in our modern times that "sex" is one of the secrets of winning men. Many girls have been led to believe that if they give themselves to a man in sex, they will keep his interest and eventually win him as a mate. The idea is not only erroneous but can be one of the most disheartening experiences a woman can have. Although it may be true that a girl who yields will win a sex partner, she will not always win a husband. Surveys show clearly that men who have sexual relations with girls, are not necessarily interested in them as mates. Of men studied in these surveys, 82% did not really love the girls they were involved with, and only 14% were really serious.

Do not base your hopes on a false premise. If a man desires you for a sex partner it will not assure you that he desires you for a marriage partner, or that he necessarily even likes you.

Sexual surrender is not one of the secrets of winning men into holy matrimony. It can, in fact, be a detriment, for good men prefer to marry girls who are pure in character. Even more serious, pre-marital sex is a serious sin in the eyes of God.

Attracting Men — An Art

Do not think that there is anything wrong with the study of winning the attentions of men, or the strategy which is necessary in winning a particular man for a mate. A girl is left alone to find her marriage partner, without the help of parents or relatives. In some cultures, and more in the past than the present, parents planned the mating of their children from early childhood. This may have had its disadvantages, but at least a girl did grow up free of the worry and responsibility of finding a mate.

In our society, a girl has much stress placed upon her with the challenge to find a husband and father for her children, in the few short years she is considered most available. I don't think we realize how some girls worry about it and many suffer because of it. Left without knowledge to guide them, some never succeed in winning the notice of men and others innocently make mistakes which drive men away. They feel "overlooked," "cast aside" and failures as women. The pain is deep and some even have had dreams about it which lasts for years, even after marriage.

It works best when man is the pursuer, the girl the object of pursuit. This is not only custom, but basic nature of the masculine and the feminine. The girl must depend upon her charm, feminine wiles and ways and even strategy to win the man she loves.

It is right and natural for every young girl to seek to be loved and to marry. She is seeking something more than just the man himself and the love that he bestows. She is seeking a life for herself, a larger and nobler life than being single offer. She wants a home of her own, a little nest to make comfortable and to warm with her love and kindness. She wants to be someone's partner and to share with him his joys and sorrows. She wants an opportunity to be a tender, loyal and devoted wife and the mother of a family. And she wants, above all, to avoid the narrower life of living alone with no one to care for, to work for, to live and to die for. In fact, to want to find the man she loves is the holiest aim a woman can entertain.

Learning the art of winning men has been rather a haphazard affair for young girls. There is little in print to guide them. The only school has been the school of experience, where lessons have been obtained at a high cost and where it is not expected that the education be complete or masterful.

Some girls, it is true, have been exceedingly fascinating and captivating, but they have relied more upon instincts to guide them than sound knowledge of basic principles. These few special charmers always do the right thing at the right time and every man they meet is more or less attracted. Other girls, though not so universally attractive, have their latent instincts for winning men aroused, when they meet a particular desirable man, who causes them to suddenly blossom out and show every evidence of real charm.

But there is a great army of girls, many of them both lovely and worthy, who cannot depend upon impulse and instinct for guidance in attracting men. Either through shyness or withdrawal from men, or through an artificial culture that has made the suppression of their natural feelings habitual, they have permitted their instincts to grow rusty. Even when nature does prompt them to do the right thing, so far as winning men is concerned, they hold back because of a typical distrust of their natural impulses or the fear of being childish. As a result, their instincts atrophy from disuse until they must depend upon something more than mere impulse for guidance in captivating men.

It is time, therefore, for a study to be made, an education offered for one of the most important areas of a woman's life — that of winning her man and building for herself a happy home.

If you will study the subject you will find yourself capable of winning the interest of many men, where before you perhaps could interest but one or two. When you meet a man who is worthy of being a lifetime partner, you will not depend upon luck or instinct for success in winning him, but will depend upon sound knowledge of basic principles, upon understanding of men's characteristics and needs and upon the practical experience of thousands of women in attracting men.

Do not think that men will mind you studying this. To find a girl who captivates him and turns his heart upside down is invigorating to a man and will give his entire life more meaning. Loving a woman is his most noble experience and marriage a part of the divine plan for him also. It is doubtful any man will mind being won by a lovable fascinating woman who would make him an ideal partner.

What this Book Can Do for You

You will learn:

❖ What men find fascinating in women

❖ The kind of woman a man wants

❖ How to awaken a man's feelings of love and tenderness

❖ How to understand men, their special needs, characteristics and vulnerable points

❖ The way to self-confidence with men

❖ How to be a good conversationalist

❖ Feminine wiles and ways

❖ The real charm that men find in women

❖ How to be adorable when angry

❖ How to make a man feel like a man

❖ Strategy with men and keys to winning them

❖ Where and how to find men

❖ Choosing a mate — what to look for

❖ The six stages of winning a man

❖ How to make men notice you

❖ Arousing his interest and love

❖ Mistakes that drive men away

❖ Sex and affection, the wise and the foolish aspects

❖ Removing the obstacles to marriage

❖ How to create romantic situations

❖ Principles of inspiring a proposal

Chapter 1
Celestial Love

Celestial love is a term I have used to describe the highest kind of tender love a man can feel for a woman. It is another name for true love, romantic love or story book love. This romantic love should be understood by all women, for it is the center of our happiness. Even in early youth, little girls have tender dreams of romance in which they are the beautiful princess who is sought after by the handsome prince. He asks for her hand in marriage and offers to give his life, if necessary, to make her happy.

Cinderella and Snow White are favorites of little girls and revered by women of all ages. This tender, storybook love is what every woman has wanted since the world began. It has always been the theme of great operas, novels and songs. Romantic love, the most moving force in life, rightfully deserves our study and consideration.

The single girl must first inspire her man to true love before he will have the courage to take the big step of marriage. Many fears stand in his way. Only the force of love will cause him to sacrifice his freedom, tax his usually limited resources and undertake the heavy responsibilities of marriage. After marriage, a girl must strive earnestly to maintain her husband's love if she is to make the ultimate success of her family life.

Young women should take courage with the thought that they can both win and maintain a man's love by following certain established principles outlined in this book.

What is romantic love? When a man loves with all his heart he experiences an intensely thrilling sensation. It has been described as a feeling almost like pain. It can cause him to feel like biting his teeth together. He feels exuberant and light, like walking in clouds. At times he feels fascinated and enchanted with the girl. Along with all of these thrilling and consuming sensations there is a tenderness, a desire to protect and shelter his woman from all harm, danger and difficulty. Then there is the deeper and spiritual feeling of worship. Even this, perhaps, cannot adequately describe the "many splendored thing" called love.

John Alden and Priscilla

There are many examples in literature of a man's deep love for a woman. In Longfellow's account of John Alden and Priscilla, John speaks tenderly of her: "There is no land so sacred, no air so pure and wholesome as is the air she breathes and the soil that is pressed by her footsteps. Here for her sake will I stay and like an invisible presence, hover around her forever, protecting, supporting her weakness." Notice that John speaks worshipfully of Priscilla and also with a tender desire to protect and shelter her from all harm.

Victor Hugo's Love – Adèle Foucher

Another illustration from literature, a tender protective feeling of love is found in the words of Victor Hugo, written about the woman he loved in real life, Adèle Foucher: "Do I exist for my own happiness? No, my whole existence is devoted to her, even in spite of her. And by what right should I have dared to aspire to her love? What does it matter, so that it does not injure her happiness? My duty is to keep close to her steps, to surround her existence with mine, to serve her as a barrier against all dangers; to offer my head as a stepping stone; to place myself unceasingly between her and all sorrows, without claiming reward, without expecting recompense.

Alas! If she only allow me to give my life to anticipating her every desire, all her caprices; if she but permit me to kiss with respect her adored footprints; if she but consent to lean upon me at times amidst the difficulties of life." Notice here again, not only do we find a protective feeling but one of worship, indicated by his desire to "kiss with respect her adored footprints."

Teddy Roosevelt's Love — Alice

President Teddy Roosevelt had a most devoted and tender love for his first wife, Alice. She died after they had been married about a year and so crushed was he that he seldom talked about her. In his diary he expressed his beautiful love for her: "Oh, how bewitchingly pretty she looked. If loving her with my whole heart and soul can make her happy, she shall be happy. The aim of my whole life shall be to make her happy and to shield and guard her from every trial. And Oh, how I shall cherish my sweet queen!" Later he writes: "I am so happy that I hardly know what to do. My own beautiful queen is the same as ever and yet, with a certain added charm that I do not know how to describe. I cannot take my eyes off her. It seems almost profanation to touch her, no matter how gently and tenderly." And still later: "It is impossible to describe the lovely little ways of my darling. I can imagine no picture so pretty as her sweet self-seated behind the tea things, in the daintiest pink and grey morning dress. She seems in beautiful health and she looks even prettier than she ever has before." Notice again the feeling is one of devotion, protection and worship.

Woodrow Wilson's Love — Ellen

Probably one of the finest examples of true and enduring love is found in the love letters of President Woodrow Wilson, written to his wife Ellen. After being married for 17 years, he writes: "All that I am, all that has come to me in life, I owe to you. I could not be what I am, if I did not take such serene happiness from my union with you. You are the spring of content; and so long as I have you, and you too are happy, nothing but good and power can come to me. Ah, my incomparable little wife, may God bless and keep you."

And after being married for 28 years he writes from the White House: "I adore you! No President but myself ever had exactly the right sort of wife! I am certainly the most fortunate man alive." And in another letter: "I can think of nothing, while I write, but only you. My days are not so full of anxiety and of a sense of deep responsibility as they are of you, my absent darling, who yet plays the leading part in my life, every minute of the day." These letters were taken from "The Priceless Gift," a collection of letters written by President Wilson to his wife Ellen. Each letter is a love letter, tender and devoted. I only bring out these illustrations to show you what a tremendous feeling romantic love really is. And at this point I want to emphasize that in every case the woman awakens these feelings. They do not just arise spontaneously within the man, without anything on the outside to spark the feelings. The woman's actions awaken his love. And this is the kind of love she must arouse if she is to bring the man to marriage. Only such an overwhelming feeling of true love can cause him to face the responsibilities which will be his for a lifetime.

Some women falsely think that only a few men are romantic and adoring, that most men are more reserved, matter of fact and practical. This is simply not true. Every man has romantic feelings that can be awakened by an adorable woman. Some still argue that even though all men have the capacity to feel tender and devoted, they are hampered by their inability to express themselves. Here again the thinking is not true. Every man can and will express his love for a woman he worships, a woman who inspires these feelings. The warm tender letters of President Wilson were a surprise to many who knew his personality, that of an unemotional schoolmaster. Is it Selfish?

A young girl's desire for devoted and tender love is not in any way selfish. In the first place she must awaken the man's love if she is to bring him to marriage, which is anything but selfish. The greatest contribution a woman can make to society is to marry, and to successfully fill her role as a wonderful wife, mother and homemaker. There is no greater aim than this. The very heart of this happy home is her marriage, which is kept together by the bonds of love. The feeling of romantic love is also a benefit to the man.

The thrilling sensation of love is a real joy to him, giving his life new meaning. He now has something to work for, to live for and if necessary to die for. Love provides him with incentive to excel and succeed in his work. He becomes a better person and feels more like a man. The woman who awakens his love brings him fulfillment whereas the woman who fails robs him of one of his finer joys.

The aim of this philosophy is to teach you the principles of winning this romantic love, principles which have been proved in thousands of cases. This is accomplished by learning to understand men, their natures, characteristics and vulnerable points and just what it is they adore in women. We will study "the kind of woman a man wants," the kind he can treasure and cherish, and then will learn how we acquire these same fascinating traits and awaken his romantic love. Every woman can be adorable if she will only rely upon her natural instincts. Perhaps your own instincts have grown rusty, but they can be awakened and make you a more fascinating woman.

Part 1

The Ideal Woman

The Kind of Woman a Man Wants

If you want to win the interest of men, it is important to know just what it is men want or admire in women. It is useless to spend time, money and energy in grooming and training yourself to be appealing to men if you do not first find out just what men feel is important. This is not easy to understand since men and women differ in their opinions of feminine appeal.

Differences in Viewpoint

In considering the charms of womanhood, women are inclined to appreciate poise, talent, intellectual gifts and cleverness of personality, whereas men admire girlishness, tenderness, sweetness of character, vivacity and the girl's ability to understand men. A marked difference in viewpoint is in regard to appearance.

Women are inclined to be attracted to artistic beauty such as the shape of the face, the nose, and artistic clothes. Good men, however, have a different interpretation of "what makes a woman beautiful." They place more stress upon the sparkle in the eyes, smiles, freshness, radiance and the feminine manner.

If you want to be attractive to men, it is important to first understand this masculine viewpoint. Rid yourself of preconceived ideas, thoughts and standards of feminine charm so that you can understand more clearly what men want, for their standards of feminine perfection are different from our own. The things that we women admire in each other are rarely attractive to men. On the other hand, the characteristics which the average woman ignores or condemns in another woman are sometimes just the characteristics which make her fascinating to men.

Women are blind to their own charms, which is the very reason it is often difficult for them to realize what a man wants. This difference in viewpoint is illustrated in Thackeray's novel Vanity Fair.

For example, Amelia, one of the leading characters in the story, was not admired by the women of her acquaintance. As one woman put it, "She is facade and insipid!" and another asks, "What could George find in that creature?" Then Thackeray adds a few observations of his own. "Has the loved reader, in his experiences of society never heard similar remarks by good natured female friends; who always wonder what you could see in Miss Smith that is so fascinating; or what could induce Major Jones to propose to that silly, insignificant, simpering Miss Thompson."

But back to Amelia. What did the men in Thackeray's novel think of her? They considered her a "kind, fresh, smiling, artless, tender little domestic goddess whom men are inclined to worship."

Haven't you been puzzled at times to know what a certain man sees in a particular girl? To you she doesn't have any appeal, yet the man may be completely enamored. The fascination men feel for certain women seems to be an eternal riddle to the rest of her sex. Even when the man is asked "why," he finds himself at a loss to explain the spell cast upon him. And haven't you also known girls who appear to have all of the qualities which ought to please a man, yet they are unnoticed, neglected and unpopular with the boys. I know a girl who was very beautiful and well dressed. Her mother spent quite a lot of money on her clothes, but they still failed to attract the young men. In moments of discouragement she would look into the mirror and say woefully, "What is wrong with you?" She was blind and could not see the missing ingredients to her charm, because she was looking at herself through a woman's eyes. This blindness on the part of women is why they spend countless hours on their appearance and may still fail to be fascinating to men. Appearance is important, but it is not all important. A woman must have a lot more to offer a man than an attractive outer shell if she is to win his heart.

If you will observe, you will see many beautiful girls who dress in the finest clothes, yet who have failed to awaken the interest or attentions of men. And if you will look further, you will see others who are not particularly attractive, as we women see it, and yet they are very much sought after by men.

In our study of the kind of woman a man wants, we must remember, then, that he judges with a different set of values. What are his values and what does he find appealing?

I will try to create in your minds an image of the kind of woman a man wants, the IDEAL WOMAN from a man's point of view. As you study these pages, try to build this image in your mind. Once you have this picture firmly established you will be drawn to it — you will tend to be this image.

You may wonder if this picture of "the ideal" does not differ in each man. Men do, of course, have different tastes. Some men want a woman who is quiet and retiring, others prefer one who is dashing and outgoing, and still others want a more dramatic or glamorous type. Some men like tall blondes; others prefer short brunettes. Some men appreciate a woman's ability to cook and sew while others insist a sense of humor is more essential. There are diverse types of men in the world and they do not all want the same kind of woman. But with all their differences, men are still alike in their basic desires.

There are certain qualities which have universal attraction and only certain ones will arouse their love. These are the qualities which we will analyze in our study of the kind of woman a man wants.

The Angelic and the Human

The kind of woman a man wants is divided into two parts. The one part is her spiritual qualifications. We will call this side of her the Angelic. The other part relates to her human characteristics; her femininity and charm, and her body and its expressions and motions. We will call this side of her Human.

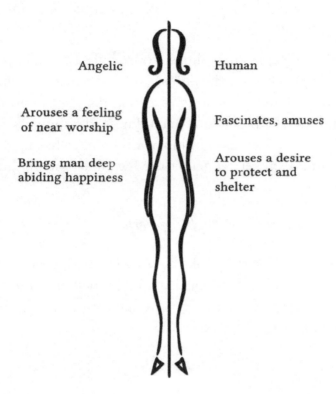

Angelic

Arouses a feeling of near worship

Brings man deep abiding happiness

Human

Fascinates, amuses

Arouses a desire to protect and shelter

The human side fascinates, amuses and arouses a desire to protect and shelter. The angelic side of woman has to do with her basic character, her ability to understand men, the responsibility she assumes in her feminine role and the many virtues that she acquires.

The human side refers to her appearance, manner and actions and includes the charms of radiance, bright eyes, smiles, delicate femininity and a quality of helpless dependency upon men for protection and guidance. Together these two qualities blended into one whole offer the perfect woman, from a man's viewpoint. They are both essential in winning his interest and love.

These two separate qualities arouse different feelings within a man's heart. The Angelic arouses a feeling near worship. The Human side, which is just as essential, fascinates and amuses men. The Angelic brings understanding and happiness to man, while the Human arouses in his heart a tender feeling, a desire to protect and shelter. Together the feeling is one of cherishing her.

David Copperfield

A perfect illustration of the Angelic and the Human in woman is in the story of David Copperfield, by Charles Dickens. Our ideal, however, is not represented by one woman, but by two, Agnes and Dora.

Agnes

Agnes represents the Angelic side of our ideal, the side which inspires worship. David Copperfield knew Agnes from childhood and worshipped her from the time he first beheld her. The following is a description of their first meeting and shows his feelings of worship.

"Mr. Wickfield (Agnes' father) tapped at a door in a comer of the paneled wall and a girl of about my age came quickly out and kissed him. On her face I saw immediately the placid and sweet expression of the lady whose picture had looked at me downstairs (her mother). It seemed to my imagination as if the portrait had grown womanly and the original remained a child. Although her face was quite bright and happy, there was a tranquility about it, and about her — a quiet good calm spirit — that I never have forgotten; that I never shall forget. 'This was his little housekeeper, his daughter, Agnes,' Mr. Wickfield said. When I heard how he said it, and saw how he held her hand, I guessed what the one motive of his life was. She had a little basket trifle, hanging at her side with keys in it, and she looked as staid and as discreet a housekeeper as the old house could have. She listened to her father as he told her about me, with a pleasant face; and when he had concluded, proposed to my aunt that we should go upstairs and see my room. We all went up together, she before us. A glorious old room it was with more oak beams and diamond panes; and the broad balustrade going all the way up.

"I cannot call to mind where or when, in my childhood, I had seen a stained-glass window in a church. Nor do I recall its subject. But I know that when I saw her turn around in the grave light of the old staircase and wait for me above, I thought of that window; and I associated something of its tranquil brightness with Agnes Wickfield ever afterwards."

David and Agnes became the closest of friends. She gave him comfort, understanding, true sympathy and comradeship. "As if," he writes, "in love, joy, sorrow, hope, or disappointment, in all emotions, my heart turned naturally there and found its refuge and best friend."

Agnes always had a sacred and peaceful influence on David. At one time, while under great stress and tension, he said, "Somehow as I wrote to Agnes on a fine evening by my open window, and the remembrance of her clear calm eyes and gentle face came stealing over me, it shed such a peaceful influence upon the hurry and agitation in which I had been living lately . . . that it soothed me into tears." But, although he had known Agnes since childhood, although he had worshipped her from the time he first beheld her, and although he senses all along that she alone is equipped to give him true sympathy and comradeship, he becomes madly infatuated not with Agnes, but with Dora.

Dora

Dora represents the Human side of our ideal, the side that fascinates, captivates and inspires an overwhelming tenderness in a man's heart and a desire to protect and shelter. David describes her in the following words:

"She was a fairy and a sylph. She was more than human to me. I don't know what she was — anything that no one ever saw and everything that everybody ever wanted. She had the most delightful little voice, the gayest little laugh, the pleasantest and most fascinating little ways that ever led a lost youth into hopeless slavery. She was rather diminutive altogether . . . she was too bewildering. To see her lay the flowers against her dimpled chin was to lose all presence of mind and power of language in feeble ecstasy."

Her childlike ways, her dear little whims and caprices, her girlish trust in him, her absolute dependency upon others to provide for her, made an irresistible appeal to David's gentlemanly and chivalrous heart. She fascinated him, for he writes: "I could only sit down before the fire, biting the key of my carpet bag, and think of the captivating, girlish, bright eyed, lovely Dora. What a form she had, what a face she had, what a graceful, variable, enchanting manner."

Married to Dora, David Turns to Agnes

Yet even while such feelings toward Dora are at their highest, he misses the comfort, the understanding, the appreciation and the sacred influences of Agnes. "Dora," he tells Agnes, "is rather difficult to — I would not for the world say, to rely upon, because she is the soul of purity and truth — but rather difficult to — I hardly know how to express it. Whenever I have not had you, Agnes, to advise and approve in the beginning, I have seemed to go wild and to get into all sorts of difficulty. When I have come to you, at last, as I have always done, I have come to peace and happiness."

Dora's Homemaking

In marriage, Dora also failed as a homemaker. Their home was in constant clutter: "I could not have wished for a prettier little wife at the opposite end of the table, but I certainly could have wished when we sat down for a little more room. I did not know how it was, but although there were only two of us, we were at once always cramped for room, and yet had always enough to lose everything in. I suspect it could have been because nothing had a place of its own." Dora could not manage the household finances, nor the household help, although she tried. Nor could she cook, although David bought her an expensive cook book. But she used the book to let her little dog stand on.

The Void in His Life

While married to Dora he continued to love her. She fascinated and amused him, and he felt tenderly towards her. But it was not a complete love, nor did it bring him genuine happiness, for he said: "I loved my wife dearly, and I was happy; but the happiness I had vaguely anticipated once was not the happiness I enjoyed, and there was something wanting. An unhappy feeling pervaded my life, as a strain of sorrowful music, faintly heard in the night." And he said, "I wished my wife had had more character and purpose to sustain me; had been endowed with a power to fill up the void which somewhere seemed to be about me." Later on in the story Dora died and David turned to Agnes.

When married to Agnes, David enjoyed real peace and happiness, for she filled up the void in his life. She was a wonderful homemaker and gave him true understanding. They had children and a wonderful home life. His love for Agnes was holy, but — it was not complete. During his marriage to Agnes he still had tender recollections of Dora that played upon his emotions. In thinking of her he writes: "This appeal of Dora's made such a strong impression on me. ... I look back on the time I write of; I invoke the innocent figure that I dearly loved to come out of the mists and shadows of the past and turn its gentle head toward me once again."

On one occasion his little girl came running in to her father with a ring on her finger very much like the engagement ring he had given to Dora. The little ring — a band of forget-me-nots, with blue stones, so reminded him of Dora, that he said, "there was a momentary stirring in my heart, like pain!"

Comparing the Two

If Agnes had had the girlishness, the adorable human and childlike manner of Dora, and her complete dependency upon man for protection and guidance, David would never have married another. His worship for Agnes would have turned into deeper, more complete love, into the desire to protect and shelter. On the other hand, if Dora had had the sympathetic understanding, the appreciation of his highest ideals and the depth of character that Agnes had, and had given his home order and peace, David's mad infatuation for her would have developed into everlasting adoration and love. Neither of the two, unfortunately for them, represents the whole of the Angelic and the Human. Each of them made mistakes, each of them won and lost David, but each of them is well worth emulating in some respects.

Analyzing Agnes

What she had:

Agnes had four outstanding qualities that appeal to men, and they are all on the Angelic side of our ideal.

1. She had a pure and lovely character, for David always associated her with a "stained-glass window of a church," and said she had a sacred influence on him. Perhaps the greatest test of her character came when David married Dora. Even though

Agnes herself loved David, she did not become bitter or resentful 1 toward either of them, but continued her unselfish friendship to David, and became a friend to Dora as well. She had the courage to keep her love a secret and to live a useful life in spite of her own disappointment. Further evidence of her character is shown in her devotion to her father and the sacrifice of many of her own pleasures for his sake.

2. Agnes understood men. She gave David true understanding. She knew how to rejoice with him in his triumphs and sympathize with him in his difficulties. She brought him comfort, peace and comradeship.

3. She was a capable housekeeper. From the time she was a child, Agnes was a "discreet little   housekeeper." She took care of the meals, the house and her father, with womanly efficiency.

4. Inner happiness. As a result of her pure character, Agnes had a "tranquility about her, and a good calm spirit," which indicates peace, or happiness within.

What Agnes Lacked:

1. She was too independent. She was too hesitant to lean on David or to need him. She was too unselfish, for David said, "Agnes, ever my guide and best support — if you had been more mindful of yourself, and less of me, when we grew up together, I think my heedless fancy never would have wandered from you."

Because she hesitated to lean on him for anything, this made her appear to be too independent. She did not appear to need his manly care and protection.

2. She lacked the girlish, childlike, trusting qualities.

3. She lacked the gentle, tender, fascinating little ways that stir a man's heart.

Analyzing Dora

What she had:

1. She had an enchanting manner.

2. She was childlike, girlish. At times he would refer to her as his "child-bride." At times she would shake her curls as little girls do. Her attitude was childlike, trusting.

3. She had tender little ways. The way she laid the flowers against her dimpled chin, or the way she patted the horses or spanked her little dog, fascinated David.

4. She was cheerful. She had a charming little laugh, a delightful little voice, and the pleasantest little ways.

5. She was bright-eyed.

6. She was dependent. She was in need of masculine protection and guidance. She had a girlish trust in David.

What Dora Lacked:

1. She was a poor homemaker. She could neither keep house, nor cook, nor manage her household expenses.

2. She lacked character. Dora was good, pure and kind, but she was very self-centered. David said, "I wished my wife had had more character and purpose to sustain me." She was too absorbed in her own little problems, cares, and whims to make a good wife.

3. She did not understand men. This was her greatest lack.

She did not know how to offer sympathy, understanding, appreciation or intellectual comradeship, for he writes, "It would have been better if my wife could have helped me more, and shared my many thoughts in which I had no partner."

The Feeling David Had for Each of Them

The feeling David had for Agnes was one near worship. She had a sacred influence on him. She brought him peace and happiness, and without her he seemed to "go wild and get into difficulty." Thinking about her "soothed him into tears." He felt as though she were a part of him, "as one of the elements of my natural home."

The feeling he had for Dora was different. She fascinated and amused him; "she was more than human to me"; "she was a fairy and a sylph"; "I don't know what she was — anything that no one ever saw and everything that everybody ever wanted." All of her delicate and bright mannerisms aroused his irresistible longing to shelter and protect her.

I would like to stress that David Copperfield felt two distinctly different types of love of these two girls. David experienced a type of love for Agnes all along, but it was not strong enough to bring him to marriage. And even though this type of love brings men the greatest peace and the truest and most abiding happiness — it is not the most driving.

The kind of love David felt for Dora was forceful, consuming and intense. He felt like "biting the key of his carpet bag" when he thought of her; he was "in fairyland." He was "a captive and a slave." This type of love, however, was not complete, nor did it bring him real happiness, for he said, "I loved my wife dearly and I was happy; but the happiness I vaguely anticipated once was not the happiness I enjoyed and there was something wanting. An unhappy feeling pervaded my life, as a strain of sorrowful music, faintly heard in the night."

While married to Agnes he experienced peace and happiness and he loved her dearly, but he still had tender recollections of Dora which sent stirring feelings through his heart. David Copperfield never had the satisfaction of loving completely, for his feelings were inspired by two different women. Neither was the whole of our ideal, so neither could arouse his love in a complete sense.

There are many women such as Agnes, in this life — women with inspiring characters. They make wonderful mothers and homemakers and are good citizens. They are greatly appreciated, but if they lack the adorably human qualities that so fascinate men, they might fail to win the interest and love of the man they hope to marry. A man wants more than an angel.

On the other hand, there are some women such as Dora, who are tender, childlike and happy little creatures, but if they have not the depth of character and purpose, if they are too self-centered to be good homemakers and mothers, and if they lack the ability to understand men, they will only win a part of a man's love.

There is no reason why a woman cannot be both an Agnes and a Dora, for the Angelic and the Human qualities do not conflict. Both are a natural part of femininity and are essential to real feminine charm. Both the Angelic and the Human qualities are essential in attracting men and in keeping them happy after marriage — thereby sustaining their love and devotion. Your complete happiness in marriage depends upon your development of both sides of our ideal.

Deruchette

An example of a girl who had both the Angelic and the Human qualities is Deruchette, heroine of the novel, Toilers of the Sea, by Victor Hugo:

In describing Deruchette, Victor Hugo first compares her to a little bird that flits from branch to branch, as she moves about the house from room to room, coming and going, stopping to comb her hair, as a bird plumes its wings, and making all kinds of gentle noises, murmurings of unspeakable delight.

She is "fresh and joyous as the lark." As one observes Deruchette, the author suggests, "one would almost be tempted to say, 'good morning, mademoiselle goldfinch.'" "She has a childlike prattle" and "she who is one day to become a mother is for a long while a child."

You may think at this point, that Deruchette is a bit insipid, as the women did of Amelia in Vanity Fair. Remember, however, that Victor Hugo was a man, a rugged man who wrote challenging sea stories, speaking more the language of men than women. But here is a peek into his masculine viewpoint of true femininity.

When the young clergyman in the story proposed to Deruchette, he gave indication of her angelic qualities when he said, "There is for me but one woman on earth. It is you. I think of you as a prayer — you are a glory in my eyes. To me you are holy innocence. You alone are supreme. You are the living form of a benediction." Then Hugo goes on to describe Deruchette further:

"Her presence lights the home; her approach is like a cheerful warmth; she passes by, and we are content; she stays awhile and we are happy. Is it not a thing of divine, to have a smile which, none know how, has the power to lighten the weight of that enormous chain that all the living in common drag behind them? Deruchette possessed this smile; we may say that this smile was Deruchette herself.

"Deruchette had at times an air of bewitching languor; and certain mischief in the eye, which were altogether involuntary. Sweetness and goodness reigned throughout her person; her occupation was only to live her daily life; her accomplishments were the knowledge of a few songs; her intellectual gifts were summed up in simple innocence; she had the graceful repose of the West Indian woman, mingled at times with giddiness and vivacity, with the teasing playfulness of a child, yet with a dash of melancholy. Add to all this an open brow, a neck supple and graceful, chestnut hair, a fair skin, slightly freckled with exposure to the sun, a mouth somewhat large, but well defined, and visited from time to time with a dangerous smile. This was Deruchette."

There is in this world no function more important than that of being charming — to shed joy around, to cast light upon dark days, to be the golden thread of our destiny and the very spirit of grace and harmony. Is not this to render a service?

Analyzing Deruchette

Her Angelic Qualities:

1. Her character. "Sweetness and goodness reigned throughout her person." She had a character which was mindful of the needs of others, for she "cast light upon dark days," and had a "smile which had the power to lighten the enormous chain." Further evidence of her character is in her lover's statement that she is "holy innocence," "is like a prayer" and the "living form of a benediction."

2. Domestic. She was capable in her domestic duties, for her occupation is only to live her daily life," and "her presence lights the home."

3. Inner Happiness. Similar to Agnes, Deruchette possessed inner happiness, or she could not possibly have had such ability to radiate it to others.

Her Human Qualities:

1. Childlikeness. Like Dora, Deruchette had childlike ways. "She who is one day to be a mother, remains for a long while a child." She had a "childlike prattle" and "certain mischief in the

eye," and at times "the giddiness and vivacity, and the teasing playfulness of a child."

2. Changefulness. Deruchette was not at all times the same. Sometimes she was radiantly happy and full of giddiness and vivacity; at other times she had an air of "bewitching languor." Although she was sweet and good, at times she had "a certain mischief in the eye." Sometimes she was full of teasing-playfulness, and at other times, "a dash of melancholy." Changefulness is also a childlike quality.

3. Fresh Appearance. "She is fresh and joyous as the lark."

4. Gentle. Her gentle qualities are described in her voice; "She makes all kinds of gentle noises, murmurings of unspeakable delight."

5. Radiates Happiness. The most notable quality she had was her ability to radiate happiness. This was a part of her character, manner and actions.

a. She was fresh and joyous as the lark.

b. She shed joy around.

c. She cast light upon dark days.

d. Her presence lights the home.

e. Her approach is like a cheerful warmth.

f. She passes by and we are content.

g. She stays a while and we are happy.

h. She has a smile which had the power to lighten the weight of that enormous chain which all the living in common drag behind them — a dangerous smile which was Deruchette herself.

i. At times she had giddiness and vivacity.

6. Grace. Not mentioned before, but similar to gentleness and tenderness is that of grace.

Deruchette was the very spirit of grace and harmony and had the "graceful repose of the West Indian woman." Her neck was supple and graceful.

Amelia

Another example in literature of a girl who was both Angelic and Human is Amelia, from the novel Vanity Fair, by Thackeray.

Thackeray says that Amelia is a "kind, fresh, smiling, artless, tender little domestic goddess, whom men are inclined to worship." A few pages further he calls her "poor little tender heart." In another place he attributes to her "such a kindly, smiling, tender, generous heart of her own." He admits that others might not consider her beautiful:

"Indeed, I am afraid that her nose was rather short, than otherwise, and her cheeks a good deal too round for a heroine; but her face blushed with rosy health and her lips with the freshest of smiles, and she had a pair of eyes which sparkled with the brightest and honestest of good humor, except indeed when they filled with tears, and that was a great deal too often; for the silly thing would cry over a dead canary, or over a mouse that the cat haply had seized upon; or over the end of a novel, were it ever so stupid."

Amelia had a "sweet, fresh little voice." She was subject to "little cares, fears, tears, timid misgivings." She trembled when anyone was harsh. Altogether, she was: "Too modest, too tender, too trustful, too weak, too much woman," for any man to know without feeling called upon to protect and cherish.

Analyzing Amelia

Amelia had several qualities worthy of our attention.

Her Angelic Qualities:

1. Her character. She had a generous heart and was kindly, and since "men are inclined to worship her," she evidently had a worthy character.

2. Her Domestic Qualities. Thackeray calls her "a little domestic goddess."

Her Human Qualities:

1. Her freshness. She had the freshest of smiles, and her face blushed with rosy health. She had a pair of eyes that sparkled. She had a sweet, fresh little voice.

2. She had childlike emotions. Her eyes would often fill with tears. She would cry over a dead canary, or a mouse or a novel. She is subject to little cares, tears, fears, timid misgivings. She trembles when anyone is harsh.

3. Tenderness. She was a "tender little domestic goddess." She was "too tender, too weak, too much woman."

4. Trustfulness. "She was too trustful."

Summary

As we come to the end of our study of these four women, we can see that there are many qualities which men admire in women. Now, I am going to blend these appealing qualities into one whole, the total woman, the kind man is inclined to worship, to protect and to cherish.

On the following page is a diagram of the total woman, with the essential qualities which men find appealing. Although she is divided, you should always think of her as one, the angelic and the human combined. Together they form the ultimate in real feminine charm.

Angela Human

Angelic Qualities

1. Understands men

2. Has deep inner happiness

3. Has a worthy character

4. Is a Domestic Goddess

Human Qualities

1. Femininity

2. Fascinates, amuses

3. Arouses a desire to protect and shelter

4. Child-like-ness

The Angelic side of woman arouses in man a feeling approaching worship. These qualities bring peace and happiness to a man.

The Human side of woman fascinates, amuses, captivates and enchants man. It arouses a desire to protect and shelter.

Together He Cherishes. Both Are Essential to His Celestial Love.

Is Beauty Necessary?

It is interesting to note that none of these authors place importance upon natural beauty. Though they go into ecstasies over the girl's smile, or the similarity of her manner to that of a bird, or the glowing health that shows in her sparkling eyes and joyous manner; though they describe at length her tenderness and childlikeness and maintain the irreproachable purity and gentleness of her character, none of these authors claims that his heroine is exceptionally beautiful to the eye.

Amelia, for example, is chubby and stout, with a very imperfect nose: "Her nose was rather short than otherwise, and her cheeks a great deal too round for a heroine." Deruchette's complexion was marred by freckles and had a mouth somewhat large. So far, in fact, are the authors from claiming beauty for these young charmers that aside from pointing out the defects mentioned, they make no attempt to describe the outward appearance. To them, as well as to most other men, the most attractive and desirable thing in a woman is not her outward beauty, but her delicate feminine manner and actions and her fresh, radiant qualities. Agnes and Dora were both beautiful girls, so David's attraction was based upon their other qualities. Admitting this, we will have to rely upon man's opinions, in guiding us to what they admire in women.

You may wonder, "How do I know if these qualities are charming to men? How can I prove these things to be true?" I must warn you — if you ask the average man to define a fascinating woman, you are apt to be disappointed. He may feel at a loss to describe his feelings in words. He only knows a charming quality when he sees it in action. It takes an author, such as I have referred to in these illustrations from classic literature to skillfully describe these attributes. Can the opinions of a few authors establish these things as true, you may wonder? If you are still in doubt, try acquiring these qualities and see for yourself how men react. Then you will be convinced.

Remember, it is possible for you to become fascinating — the kind of woman a man wants, as described in this chapter. This goal is attainable, regardless of the attributes you were born with and your personality and character as they are now. You can take upon yourself finer qualities, greater charm and allurement which will aid you in winning a desirable man.

When Men Marry Girls Who Seem Unattractive

Now and then we will see an especially eligible and attractive man marry a girl who, to all the rest of us, appears to lack the qualities of feminine charm. They do not seem feminine, girlish, radiant, nor do they display any special merit of character. This frequently causes the question to arise, "what on earth can he see in her?" The answer is this: Just because a woman acts a certain way with all others is no reason for expecting she acts the same way for her man. Perhaps the man happened to surprise her in a moment when she had forgotten to put on her "company manner" and had acted rather childlike and cheerful. Or she may have portrayed a ray of angelic character that only he has detected. When he learns of this aspect of her nature, he is justified in feeling that he has discovered a woman of true charm.

An illustration of this may be of a woman who appears to everyone very businesslike and efficient, with a strong aggressive nature. She does not appear to anyone to be tender, feminine or childlike. Suddenly, however, a man comes along who appears to her a real hero. In the presence of what she thinks is his masterful strength, she feels as if her abilities, her efficiency, determination and vigor are small compared to his. At an unguarded moment she lets her manner and actions betray this feeling and the man's face lights up with interest. "What a delightful creature she really is," he thinks. "How mistaken I have been about her."

The sad part of this situation is that women, who tend to suppress their charm with an exterior of efficiency, may never have a man discover their true beauty. Many such women go through an entire life without a single man ever realizing their womanliness within. Such is the predicament of thousands of women who suppress their natural femininity and childlikeness. They think it impossible for them to act like the girls that usually attract men. You can rest assured, however, that these qualities are at the bottom of every woman's nature, placed there when she was born a woman and that they can be brought out either by her meeting with a particular man or by the exerting of her own determination to make herself a feminine woman.

Introduction to Understanding Men

The first quality of Angela Human is that of understanding men. Think of it as a definite quality, an ability to understand a man's characteristics, peculiarities and vulnerable points and to understand his special needs as a man.

Men are Different

The first thing to understand is that men are different from women — so different in nature and temperament that it is almost as though they came from another planet. Men do not think like women do, approach a problem in the same light, nor do they have the same sense of values or the same needs as we do. For example, the most central need a woman has is to be loved, whereas a man's most central need is to be admired. Because we fail to understand these differences we often supply men with the thing we need rather than the things they need. What are these needs?

Men's Needs

A man needs someone to talk freely to, someone to confide in, and someone to run to in times of difficulty and in moments of achievement. He needs to have someone to rely upon, someone who will be his refuge and best friend. He needs sympathy in times of despair and hope for the future — someone who can heal his wounds and restores his self-esteem. He needs someone who will accept him for the man he is and who can perceive his truth worth. If a woman can be "all of this" to a man, she becomes indispensable to his happiness and is apt to be the "one woman in his life." Of course, it is not easy to win a man's confidence so that he will rely upon you as his refuge and best friend. But the art of knowing how to get a man to confide is also one of the keys to understanding men and one which will be taught in this book.

Agnes

Agnes had the ability to understand men. David turned to her again and again, both in difficulty and triumph, for he writes: "Whenever I have not had you, Agnes, to advise and approve in the beginning, I have seemed to go wild and to get into all sorts of difficulty. When I have come to you, at last, as I have always done, I have come to peace and happiness." And in another place, "As if, in love, joy, sorrow, hope or disappointment, in all emotions, my heart turned naturally there and found its refuge and best friend."

Dora

Dora did not have this ability to understand men, for David writes: "I did sometimes feel, for a little while, that I could have wished my wife had been my counselor . . . had been endowed with power to fill up the void which somewhere seemed to be about me." And further on: "It would have been better for me if my wife could have helped me more and shared my many thoughts in which I had no partner." We will now devote ourselves to a study of men, their needs and feelings, their characteristics, peculiarities and their vulnerable points, so that we will be prepared to give them understanding. The following are the six characteristics of men, essential for any woman to know if she is to be able to understand men.

Six Characteristics of Men

1. His need to be accepted at face value

2. His need to be admired

3. His sensitive pride

4. His reserve

5. His need for sympathetic understanding

6. His need in his role as man

Chapter 3

Accept a Man at Face Value

Characteristics No. 1

The most basic thing to understand about a man is his need to be accepted at face value — accepted for the man he is. If you are seriously considering marrying a man, this is something that will be essential. This means we accept his ways; his hopes and dreams. We accept his ideas, his standards and his habits (both good and bad). We accept the little quirks in his personality, his religious views, and his political views and any traits he may have, for better or for worse. We are doing more than accepting him — we are accepting his right to be himself. We may not agree with his ideas, but we respect his right to his own viewpoint. We may notice his weaknesses, but we accept this as normal in human beings. We accept him for the man he is and look to his better side. When you are dating is the time to really decide if you love him enough to accept him as he is.

Don't make the mistake of trying to remake a man into something he is not or to offer little suggestions and hints for his self-improvement. It may be all right for others to offer him constructive criticism, in the spirit of love and kindness, but not the girl he has romantic feelings for. The woman he loves must be willing to accept him at face value. In fact, to offer any indication that you are not satisfied with him just as he is may be the very thing that will discourage a man and drive him away.

It is an even greater mistake to expect to remake a man after marriage. This will only lead to trouble, for men will resist any effort on the part of their wives to make them over. It will lead to serious marriage problems that can even destroy the relationship. If you cannot accept a man as he is, it is better to face this fact and look for someone that you can accept. This makes "acceptance" an important consideration in the step of selecting a mate.

What Does Accepting a Man at Face Value Mean?

In the business world, "face value" has a specific meaning. It is the amount a bond or an insurance policy, etc., is worth today, or now. If held a number of years it would or could be worth a good deal more, but it does have a specific value now. And what does "face value" mean in reference to a man? It means what he is worth today, just as he exists now, with no changes made.

"Accepting a man at face value" means that we recognize him as a human being who, like ourselves and all other humans, is part virtue and part fault. It is a very honest approach. We realize that the faults are there, but we are not concerned about them, for we accept the total man. If he wants to change on his own, that is his business. We are satisfied with him as he is.

Acceptance does not mean tolerance, or "putting up with faults." Nor does it mean dishonesty — that we must convince ourselves that he is perfect, when he is not. Nor does it mean resignation. When you accept a man, you see him as a total man and are content with what you see and prove your contentment by not trying to change him. Realize fully then, girls, if you want a truly romantic marriage, you will have to accept your man as he is and not expect to change him after marriage. With this thought in mind, use the utmost caution in selecting a mate — a man that you can accept as he is, with no changes.

His Need for Freedom

A man has a strong masculine nature of wanting to hold on to his freedom, even to the point of resentment. He wants to be the kind of man he wants to be and do the things he wants to do and think the way he wants to think, etc. This does not mean that he does not respect the viewpoints of others, but it does mean that he does not like being "pushed." Especially does he not like being pushed by the woman he loves.

His Need for Religious Liberty

When considering the serious step of marriage, it is wise to recognize the importance of religious freedom. Each individual has a right to his own religious views; it is our God-given right. Our nation was founded upon the principle of religious liberty.

The pilgrims left Europe because of it, and it is still just as important to each one of us today.

We do not have a right to expect another individual to adopt our viewpoint, or to make him feel obligated to do so. We can teach and inspire by example or instruction but pushing our religious views onto someone else is a mistake, one which denies the individual the right to believe as he wishes and one which will surely lead to trouble in a relationship. When we do extend to another his right to religious liberty, his mind will function without barriers and he will be much more apt to be "open to religious viewpoints." Let me illustrate by the following experience.

Some Wise Counsel

A girl was engaged to marry a man of a different religion than her own. Her religion was very important to her and she hoped that if she married him he would eventually join her church. She sought counsel from a wise man who told her, "If you do marry this man, make nothing of his religious differences to him openly. Do not attempt to change his views, but rather recognize his religious freedom. If he wants to go to his church, go with him. Give him complete freedom but hold to your ideals and be the living example of what your religion teaches."

She did marry the man and she followed the wise man's advice. He did ask her to attend his church with him which she did willingly. In return, he was willing to attend hers. By comparing the two he soon became convinced that his wife's church was superior to his own and he became a member of it.

However, if he had not accepted it, this young woman was prepared to have a difference of viewpoint when it came to religion. She had first decided to accept him no matter what, so no matter the outcome, there was no friction.

The way to acceptance is this. Respect a man's freedom to be himself and do the things he wants to do and think the way he wants to think. Accept him for the man he is, overlook his human weaknesses, failures and faults and look to his better side.

A single girl in love may not feel this is a problem. When romance is in bloom, love is most often blind. She may feel he has no faults; at least she cannot see them. The young man may add to this blindness by "putting his best foot forward" and hiding his faults, which is only human nature for him to do. If such a blind state could continue after marriage, no problems in regard to "faults" would arise, but unfortunately we sometimes notice faults in a man after marriage as our husbands "relax" their better side and tend to be themselves.

The best way to avoid such a rude awakening is to take a good look at him before marriage and know just what it is you are going to have to accept. Get to know him by long hours of conversation. Ask questions on important topics. Find out his religious views, his views about family life and his standards and ideals. Talk to him about the future so that you will know his goals — his aspirations. Take a lot of time to get to know him. There is nothing like a period of time to reveal a person's "true self." Eventually those little faults which may have been obscure will become evident. This does not mean that you will not continue to respect him and to love him, but it does mean that you will be aware of what he is and what you will have to accept. You may have to force yourself to take a good look, but it will pay. You will then be able to judge for yourself if he is a man that you can accept. If you can't accept him as he is, it might be best to end the romance and look for a companion better suited to you.

Is There Ever a Time When I Should Not Accept the Man I Love?

There is never a time that you should not accept the man you love, (unless of course, he is abusive, criminal or an unrecovered substance abuser) but there are several occasions when you should respond to his faults in a certain way. Let me explain:

1. When He is Blind to His Own Mistakes Sometimes a man is blind to his own mistakes and such blindness causes him to get into difficulty with his associates or friends and even fail to reach success. On these occasions it is only right for the woman he loves to open his eyes. Take for example the salesman who uses a poor approach, or the department supervisor who is too dictatorial, or the student who is losing out because he offends the teacher, or even a man who is losing his friends because he has body odor. In these instances, a woman should at least try to gently alert a man. Often others who observe his mistakes are not interested enough to awaken him or may feel it is not their business to do so. She may be the only one who cares enough about him to help.

The way to do it is this: Keep in mind that you do accept him. It is the world that does not! Others are offended, not you. Tell him that you have a few ideas that might prove helpful. Let him know that you are not close to the situation as he is and that you could be wrong, but "could this be the cause of his trouble." Assure him that you admire him and isn't it regrettable that others do not esteem him for his true worth. Once you have opened his eyes, do not persist in the matter. Drop it completely. If he continues to make mistakes, fully aware of them, you will have to allow him this freedom.

2. When he is Thoughtless. Must you accept a man at face value when he is thoughtless, and just overlook it? I am referring to times when he may be inconsiderate or unfair. A man is entitled to many freedoms, but he does not have the right to be unkind. You are a human being worthy of the highest respect and consideration, and it is important to both of you, and to your relationship, that you maintain your self-dignity. It is, in fact, difficult for a man to feel kindly towards a woman whom he can mistreat. Knowing how to handle these difficult situations is one of the charming arts of Fascinating Womanhood and will be taught in a later chapter.

3. When a Man Does Something that Shows Lack of Character. Another time to react to a man's faults is when he does something dishonest or sinful, showing a lack of character. You may be well aware of his better side and feel that you do accept him at face value, but if you now completely overlook his misdeed, it displays a weakness in your own character. The way to respond to his improper conduct is this:

At first show reluctance to believe it. Say that you thought it was impossible for a man such as he to do such a thing. If you are compelled to believe it, indicate that you know it is contrary to his true nature, and was only the result of carelessness or thoughtlessness. You must be immensely disappointed at his temporary lapse, but your faith in his better side must be unshaken.

Don't Fall Onto His Level

When a man shows his weaker side, as we have just mentioned, there may be a temptation for the woman to lower her standards to meet his. She may feel that she will cause the man to feel "more accepted" in this way. This is a serious mistake! He will not respect her for it. A man likes to consider a woman as "better and holier" than himself and therefore it would be a disappointment to him to see her fall from her level onto his. He cannot consider her an angelic character unless she holds to her ideals and maintains her high standards.

How a Woman Tries to Change a Man

Many disagreeable girls make the mistake of offering pushy suggestions or blunt remarks that drive men away. But more often than not, girls are subtler in their approach to men. They are more apt to drop a gentle hint or give a carefully worded suggestion about how the man needs to improve. Even though these latter forms may sound more acceptable, they are nevertheless offensive to the man and will most likely interfere with his feelings for her.

A man is sensitive to any attitude a girl may have towards him. Any thought that he is not acceptable just as he is may drive him away. You may not make these mistakes with your men friends, but since you probably live around your father, brothers, etc., it is wise to learn as much as possible about this subject and apply it to all men you associate with. There will be a number of rewards if you do. In the first place, you will promote a much better relationship with men in this way. Your brothers will be apt to want to socialize with you; maybe go to a movie, and your father will be much more willing to do things for you. There will be a much better feeling between you. The second reward is that you will begin to form habits that will help you in your associations with men for the rest of your life, not only with the man you may wish to marry, but with your own sons. Then, third, you will help all men in your life to be better men. As you look to their better side you will help them to grow into finer manhood. Important also is that you express your acceptance of the men in your life, especially those you live with. Tell your father or brothers that you are happy they are the kind of men they are.

Then look to their good qualities. The following are steps to remember in learning to accept men, just as they are:

Steps to Acceptance

1. Get rid of any self-righteous attitude.

2. Don't try to remake men, improve them, give pushy advice, drop hints or subtle suggestions about how they need to improve.

3. Don't use other men as examples.

4. Look to his better side.

5. Express your acceptance in words:

    a. Tell him that you are happy he is the kind of man he is.

    b. Express appreciation for his good qualities.

Chapter 4
Admiration

Characteristic No.2

The center of a woman's happiness is to be loved, but the center of man's is to be admired.

Deep in his heart every man longs for admiration — of his abilities, his ideas and his dreams. This admiration is his greatest happiness, and lack of it one of his most distressing miseries. Although it is all important to him, it isn't something which he can get for himself. It must be given him by those who respect and love him. He likes receiving it from any and every source, but it is most essential from the woman he loves.

A man will often do and say things deliberately in the presence of a woman, hoping to receive admiration. But these things often go unnoticed. Usually a woman is too busy or too mentally occupied with her own world and problems to notice this need. We don't often bother to find out what is in a man's heart, what he thinks and dreams about. The woman who offers the perfect admiration is the woman who wins his heart and soul.

The Young Boy

This need is manifest in the young boy and is essential to his confidence and growth into manhood. It helps him to experience love from his parents. Unfortunately, there are many young boys whose parents fail to admire them. A life of correction without praise some young men endure, but the longing is always there. When such a boy matures, he needs admiration more than ever, for doing without it in his youth has caused a lack of confidence. If the woman he marries can offer the needed admiration, his troubles are over. If not, he often becomes a lonely creature.

The Young Ambitious Man

Especially is the need for admiration apparent in the young married man just beginning his career. He expects to be an all-conquering success; no project is too wild, no dream too fantastic. He is full of plans and proposals, assurance and enthusiasm. What he doesn't expect to do, after a little preliminary preparation, of course, simply isn't worth doing. He can find a hundred flaws in the way older heads are managing things now — but you just wait until he gets his chance and revolutionizes matters. Meantime, life isn't worth living if he can't find someone to whom he can tell all this, how things ought to be, how they will be when he gets his chance.

Most of his youthful associates are too much occupied with their own aspirations to listen to his. Older people will only laugh at him. Where can he find an uncritical listener and confidante? The cry of his soul is for admiration. A woman who can give it to him is no less than an angel.

The Older Man

As a man grows older, if he has not been admired, he often learns to do without it. He becomes, it would seem, hardened, incredulous, and less sensitive to the lack of admiration. The older a man becomes, however, the more bitterly he resents this apparent indifference to the bigger and nobler elements of his character. He represses his craving for admiration because he does not believe it is to be had, but the craving for it is just as strong and persistent as it is in the younger man.

What He Wants You to Admire

What a man wants you to admire more than anything else are his manly qualities. If you admire traits which are admirable in both men and women, he will be disappointed. For example, if you admire him because he is kind, thoughtful, pleasant or well groomed, he may appreciate your praise, but it will do little to really stir him, or affect any romantic feelings towards you. It is his masculinity that he wants noticed and admired.

Physically his manly qualities are his large build, his strong muscles, his endurance, his deep pitched voice, his heavy jaw, his manly beard, his mustache, his heavy walk, his large hands, etc. We see his manly strength and endurance at work in sports, weight lifting, swimming, lifting heavy objects, managing difficult equipment, sawing logs, taming horses and even some of the more common things such as mowing the lawn, painting, opening tight jar lids, turning screws or wielding a hammer. Men's clothes are also a part of the physical. They are heavier, rougher and more tailored than women's — and therefore masculine.

Mentally his manliness lies in his achievements, skills and abilities, his judgment, cleverness, determination and his leadership ability. His manliness is also demonstrated in his hopes and aspirations for his future and his striving to reach these goals. We see masculinity in the student who achieves in his school work, the mechanic, the salesman, the carpenter, the doctor, the lawyer and all of the other fields men engage in. We see manly skills at work in repairing motors, winning a debate or receiving some honor for outstanding service or some talent displayed. The man who faithfully goes to work from day to day to provide for his family, fulfilling his role as a man, is due admiration for his efforts.

Spiritually his manliness is demonstrated in his sense of honor and duty in men's affairs, his courage and devotion to a cause, his sense of fair play, his noble deeds, his standards and aspirations or any high ideals which have to do with a man's life. Few men possess all of the masculine traits mentioned, but all men possess some of them. These are the ones we should notice and admire.

Why is admiration of masculinity so important to a man? Because it makes him feel manly and this realization of his masculinity is one of the most enjoyable feelings a man can experience. When a woman supplies him with the much-needed admiration she becomes indispensable to his happiness, and he will seek her out again and again for the comfort her companionship gives to him — the feeling of manliness he experiences in her presence. In fact, one of the keys to a man's heart is admiration of his masculinity.

Ways to Admiration

There may be a number of things which you can readily notice to admire about a man, especially those physical traits which are so apparent. But some of the finer traits may be obscure and difficult to know, especially if your acquaintance has been rather brief or superficial. You must know something about him before you can admire him, and you must know a great deal about him if you are to appreciate him for his true worth. The following are suggestions to help you discover his admirable traits:

1. Observe Him. The first thing to do is to observe him. If you will keep your eyes and ears open you will notice many things about him which are manly, things you may have formerly overlooked.

2. Listen to Others. Try to make a point to listen carefully to people who know him well. You can deliberately open a conversation with his close friends and family. Do not be too inquisitive but steer the conversation into subjects which will reveal his nature and accomplishments.

3. Listen to Him Talk. The greatest opportunity you will have to admire him is when he talks — about subjects he is interested in or about himself. These conversations will reveal many things worthy of admiration. If a man has a good

listener, he will enjoy talking. The following advice will help you become a good listener.

How to Listen to a Man

Follow this rule and you can be a good listener: Do not listen only to what he is saying, but to the man who is saying it. If he is talking about politics, religion or world events, notice how absorbed he is in the subject. As his ideas unfold, look for idealism and devotion to the things he believes in. If his attitude shows impatience with how things are, this may be an indication that he has ideas of his own, ideas which need to be expressed and appreciated. He may display a special knowledge about a subject, knowledge which comes from intelligence, experience or dedicated study.

If you cannot comprehend all of what he is saying, look for the traits of his character which you can admire. His conversation will reveal them. In fact, if you only follow his subject and appreciate that, and not the man who is thus expressing himself, he will be apt to be disappointed. You may rest assured that he is not talking only to have his subject appreciated. He wants admiration to be bestowed upon himself as a man and not merely upon his subject.

A woman need not be educated in his field to follow a clever man's discourse. In his pleasure at having himself admired the man seldom notices that his conversation is not completely understood. Even when he does notice it, he relishes it as in the following words by Maeterlinck:

What care I though she appear not to understand?

Do you think it is for a sublime word I thirst?

When I feel that a soul is gazing into my soul?

If you learn to listen to a man correctly it doesn't matter if the subject is interesting or dull. You can converse on world affairs or the intricate details of his business career and you will be able to maintain an interest. In fact, you can safely guess that if he deliberately talks "over your head" he is doing so only to arouse your admiration. If you have studied and do know a lot about his discourse, so much the better.

If you once get the habit of looking for the masculinity in the men you meet, you will not find any of them uninteresting. You will welcome the most tedious monologue as giving you an opportunity to observe the man's character, and to seek out his admirable qualities. You will develop into a most appreciative listener and will invite, unconsciously almost, the confidences of nearly every man with whom you converse.

Remember too, that if you can't see anything manly in him, he won't see anything womanly in you. It is the manly things that you are to look for in him, the manly things that you are to appreciate. The greatest attraction of the exceptionally feminine woman is that she can observe and admire the masculinity of every man she meets. She is constantly on the lookout for it.

Chapter 5
His Sensitive Pride
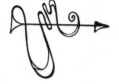

Characteristic No. 3

We have just learned of the man's great need to be admired — to be admired for his masculine abilities, skills, ideas and achievements. Now we must learn that a man is very proud of his masculine abilities. He likes to show them off, to call your attention to them in both conversation and actions. Like every male creature from the peacock and the rooster to the bull and the lion, he likes to parade before the female of the species and show what manly powers are his.

Although a man is proud of his masculinity and longs to have it noticed and appreciated, it is here he is most vulnerable for his manly pride is extremely sensitive. He cannot bear to have it belittled, ridiculed or treated with indifference. When a man is belittled, he suffers the pains of humiliation. It can be a sharp cutting sensation or a crushing feeling. Whatever the forms of humiliation, it is a painful experience.

You will remember that admiration gives a man a wonderful feeling of manliness, and in turn he feels tenderly towards the woman who makes him feel this way. Well, when this same masculinity, instead of being appreciated, is belittled, or treated with indifference, the man experiences an opposite feeling — a feeling of lack of manliness — and in turn he will not feel kindly towards the woman who makes him feel this way. Take every precaution not to do or say anything which will injure his pride, for nothing will more quickly drive a man away.

Mistakes Some Girls Make

Don't make the mistake of making fun of a man's mustache or beard, or anything to do with his masculine appearance. Be equally careful not to belittle any of his accomplishments such as grades, term papers, sports events, the way he repairs a motor, his knowledge of certain subjects or even certain high goals he may have. Often girls tend to belittle men in the form of humor. In this case it may be difficult to detect the boy's hurt pride, for he may pretend to laugh to cover up the pains of humiliation. This only obscures her mistake and as a result she is apt to repeat it again and again.

The most common cause of hurt pride, however, is an attitude of indifference. In other words, when a man reveals some masculine accomplishment or skill, the woman may show a lack of interest towards it. She may indicate by a yawn, an expression or a glance out the window that she is not impressed. If the man happens to be telling her of something of which he is particularly proud, her indifference to his masculinity can wound him as if he were struck by a lash. It is not difficult to imagine, then, how he feels towards a woman who has injured the most sensitive part of his nature and robbed him of his manliness.

Mistake of Others

Women are not the only contributors to men's humiliation. In the working world his pride may be brutally cut down. His ability may be questioned. In some companies, ridicule is common. Some sadistic employers may undermine an employee. Then there is a struggle for position in which men sometimes discredit one another. Often it is a creditor or customer who offers cutting remarks. Some workers are derided by their superiors.

On the campuses, in the classroom we sometimes observe further humiliation. Professors or fellow students are sometimes insensitive to manly pride, although they are vulnerable themselves. In sports, men freely belittle one another. This is because they tend to build themselves up by tearing others down. When we see what a man puts up with in the world with his fellow associates, it seems inexcusable for women to further add to the pains of humiliation. Women, in fact, can restore manly pride, and must, if they are to be indispensable to a man's happiness.

In speaking of the mistakes women make and the seriousness of belittling remarks and injured pride, tragedies have occurred because of it. Let me tell you of one such instance:

Belittled

Many years ago, I knew a girl who was engaged to marry a man of outstanding ability. He appeared to love her dearly but broke the engagement and married someone else. For years, it seemed a mystery to those who knew the couple, but later I learned the truth. She lost him because she belittled him. She laughed at his big ideas, made fun of his actions on the basketball court and joked about his performance in plays. Such a constant eroding of his pride was more than he could stand. This man has become extremely successful.

We have learned thus far that a man needs desperately to be admired for his masculinity and that it is indeed the "cry of his soul." He is very proud of these manly qualities, but also very sensitive about them and cannot bear to have them belittled, ridiculed or treated with indifference. If you intend to become our ideal of Angela Human and offer to a man the perfect understanding and influence his feelings towards you, it is important that you realize fully his nature and never commit the unpardonable sin of ridicule or indifference. Such an act is apt to drive him away completely. If he does overlook a single act, he is not apt to demonstrate patience if it is repeated again and again. If you do have this habit of belittling men, or showing indifference, it is essential that you rid yourself of this tendency or you will make little progress in winning the attentions of men.

Chapter 6

His Reserve

Characteristic No. 4

A reserve is a barrier that a man builds around himself, making it difficult to win his confidence. By reserve we do not mean bashfulness or timidity. The latter peculiarities apply to comparatively few men. Reserve, on the other hand, is an attribute of almost all.

In order to understand reserve, we must again refer to the subject of admiration. We have learned that to admire a man fully we must listen to him talk, so that we can observe the finer parts of his character and we will have an opportunity to admire these traits. But it is not easy to win a man's confidence so that he will talk about subjects that are near and dear to his heart. The reason for this is that his reserve stands in his way; it protects him and causes him to hesitate and withhold confidences.

This reserve is caused by fears or negative past experiences; the desire to avoid ridicule, contempt and indifference — those things that we learned about in connection with a man's pride.

Because of fears, he forms a wall of reserve which makes it difficult to get him to talk about deep feelings. Although he may long to confide, so that he can be appreciated for his masculinity, he hesitates because of his reserve, or his fear of ridicule. Nothing is so frightening to a man as the horror of making a fool of himself.

A very ambitious or intelligent man is most reluctant to expose his intimate secret hopes and ideas to indifference or antagonism. The fear of such humiliation is nothing less than appalling to him. He therefore sternly subdues every impulse to seek admiration by forming this wall of reserve. Nothing but the absolute certainty that his ideas will not be met with contempt or indifference will induce him to throw off his armor of reserve and reveal to others the things that mean the most to him. And even if he does dare, the slightest hint of misunderstanding or disrespect will shatter the illusion and drive him behind his wall of reserve again.

In order to understand the delicateness of the situation, take an example of a young girl who has successfully won a young man's confidence and he is unfolding his secret hopes and dreams. As he begins to reveal the finer traits of his character she has a most wonderful opportunity to acknowledge these manly qualities. Let her indicate by a yawn or a glance out the window that she is not interested, and the poor man will pull away. It may be the first time in his life he has ventured to express his feelings. To him, therefore, the confession is a matter of prime importance over which he has probably pondered for days. The ideas themselves, and the motives underlying them, have long been the mainspring of his being. If the girl looks indifferently upon such a crisis and fails to recognize its significance to him she has indeed so far as he is concerned a heart of stone. Therefore, no matter where or when he meets her in the future, he will not again risk a similar rebuff.

Such is the case with every man. His longing for understanding, great as it is, is not sufficient to make him throw off his habitual cloak of reserve except in rare instances. And even then, he will quickly resume it again unless he can bask in the full glow of an all comprehending understanding. The one characteristic, therefore, seems to be directly opposed to the other. Together they constitute a problem difficult enough to tax any girl's wits.

If you are to win the interest of men, you will have to first gain his trust so that he will confide his innermost feelings to you and you will be able to admire his masculinity, as has been explained. There are a number of things you can do to remove this reserve. They are the following:

How to Be Allowed Behind the Wall of Reserve

1. Accept Him. If you give any indication that you are not satisfied with him just as he is, he will not feel like exposing his innermost feelings to your unappreciative attitude.

2. Admire His Masculinity. Your admiration will do more to break down his reserve than any effort you can make.

3. Don't Belittle Him or Show Indifference. Make sure you do not make mistakes which only strengthen the reserve he already has.

4. Don't be Critical of Others. If you are scornful, with an eye open for every fault you can find in those around you, he will be afraid to expose his own intimate feelings to your criticism and contempt. When you are with him don't tell him about your quarrels with your acquaintances and about your poor opinion of this or that person. You must not betray envy or jealousy or contempt. Don't make light of anyone. Even when you cannot approve of what someone does or says, you must show your appreciation for his motives or basic character. The more ability you can manifest as a critic, the less inclined the man will be to expose himself to your criticism. He likes to believe that his confidences will meet with a generous and admiring interpretation, not with a faultfinding one.

5. Appreciate the Good in Others. If you appreciate the good in others, he will not fear ridicule or contempt when he confides his ideals and ambitions to you; he will begin to confide things about himself without any invitation on your part. Search for the good in everyone you meet and express your appreciation of them. This is the easiest way to develop a beautiful confidence-inspiring character. Unless you do this, it will be impossible for you to become Angela Human, the woman who is most attractive to good men.

6. Hold Confidences Sacred. You must hold sacred the thoughts and feelings of others, and not confide in him matters that other people have confided in you. If you disclose the secrets of others, he might take for granted that you will disclose his also and thus subject him to the same misunderstanding, ridicule or indifferences that he seeks to avoid. Unless he thinks that he is confiding his innermost

hopes and ambitions to one who will not betray them to others, most men will not confide them to you no matter how sure he is of your personal admiration of him. Even though he knows you admire him, how does he know others will? They might ridicule the things you admire. He does not want to risk the contempt of anyone. In your associations with him, then, you must not uncover secrets which have been told to you in confidence.

When the man does disclose something about himself which you can admire, do not imagine that he will open wide his wall of reserve for you. You need to make certain that everything he confides to you is met with admiration. Otherwise his first confidences will never be followed by another. If your response is always appreciative, he will add another confidence and another until at last, if your reaction is never disappointing, he will lay bare before you every motive, ideal and hope that stirs within him, though some of this will naturally be after you are married and he is able to trust you even more.

Remember, however, underlying the desire for admiration is always lurking that old wall of reserve, ready to spring out at the first sign of indifference or criticism, even when the criticism is only apparent in the girl's attitude towards other people. You can therefore understand how difficult it is for a girl with a weak, faultfinding or indifferent character to keep the reserve in the background and to maintain the man's interest.

Chapter 1

Sympathetic Understanding
Characteristic No. 5

A man needs sympathy in a number of ways, and they are the following:

1. His Responsibilities as a Man. A woman ought always to understand the responsibilities a man faces in his future. Since most men plan to marry, they have, at least in the back of their minds, a picture of what this responsibility entails. They know that they will be faced with the social and economic responsibility of a wife and children for a lifetime. They also know that their family will look to them to be their guide and protector, and that they must grow into manhood if they are to fulfill this position. They may not spend a great amount of time worrying about it, but they are nevertheless aware of it. They know that if they are to succeed in this role as man, they must make adequate preparation. With men — their college, career or their jobs are serious business. If they fail, they fail in their preparation for the future.

Success in life is at stake. They must succeed if they are to fulfill their roles as men and provide for loved ones adequately.

Now the main reason a woman needs to understand masculine responsibility is this: Men sometimes become depressed about their futures and at such times need the confidence and reassurance of a woman. They need to know that someone believes in them — believes in their ultimate success. Another reason a woman needs to understand is that this responsibility a man faces about his future can sometimes be a difficult obstacle to marriage. He may give evidence of desiring marriage and yet hesitate because of the responsibility he faces. A woman, if she knows what he is experiencing, can be a comfort to him and help remove this barrier to marriage, as will be explained in a later chapter.

2. His Desire for Status. A second way we need to understand a man's needs for sympathy is in his desire for status. By status we mean a position of honor or acclaim. Man has within his nature the drive to excel, or to shine out brightly, or to do something of note which will set him apart from other men.

This is true, not only in the human male, but in male members of the animal kingdom. The pecking order in the barnyard, the hierarchy in a colony of baboons and the ranking within a herd of elephants is more of a driving force for the male than is the sex function. Men also have the longing to take their place in the world of men. This drive for superiority over other men is a masculine trait. Women desire appreciation but they seldom have tendencies to gain superiority over one another.

He Wants to be a Hero in Your Eyes

Not only does a man want status in the eyes of the world, but more than anyone else, he wants to impress the woman he loves or is interested in. He wants to be a hero in her eyes. He may win the acclaim of the whole world, and all of the honors of earth, and yet would be disappointed if he could not impress the woman he loves. So, in your associations with men do not make the mistake of using another man as a perfect example. Do not refer to your brother, or your father or some man in the community as the model of manhood. Do not even extol some admirable man in history. Do not give some other man the acclaim that the man you love would like to receive, the acclaim of a hero. He may not have earned such honor yet, but he would like to feel that other men are not a competition to him in your eyes. He would like to feel that it would be possible for him to impress you as the perfect example of manhood.

And even worse, do not allow yourself to be a competition to his acclaim. Do not deliberately excel him in any of the fields in which he is trying to win acclaim. If you are the one who stands out as notable among your fellow co-workers — the one who has won the honor and acclaim, this is a threat to the position he hopes one day to win. We see this problem apparent with many famous women, especially movie and stage actresses. If they marry men who can outdo them, either in the field of acting or in any other occupation, then things are in their rightful place, but if men simply cannot meet the competition of their wife's acclaim, it might become a threat to his ego and can make him most uncomfortable and unhappy.

How can he impress you with his meager efforts if you have already won the honors of earth, or if he is convinced that you can or will in the future? Be particularly careful, then, of the male ego, and the inborn desire for acclaim or status and never appear as a threat to this position or allow another to appear as a threat. Man's ego is vulnerable, and therefore it is here that we can either build or destroy.

In man's drive for status try to understand his desire to impress the world and also you. He wants money and security, yes, but he also wants honor and acclaim, especially for you. He does not expect it before he has earned it, but he expects you to recognize his promise for the future, that one day he will achieve the goals he has set. This struggle for status explains the added preparation a man feels he must make while he is young. It also explains why some men later on in life become dissatisfied with a job that provides money and security, but little acclaim. It helps us to understand and sympathize with a man's striving for achievements as he goes along — the badge of merit, the champion cup and the honorary award.

3. Sympathy for the Discouraged Man. A man has a special need for sympathy when he is discouraged. Whether rich or poor, handsome or homely, learned or ignorant, few men escape this unpleasant experience. In fact, the more learned, talented and aggressive men tend to have the most intense suffering. Abraham Lincoln had periods of depression, in which he merely sat and brooded and read the newspapers. Many men of great responsibility have periods of real discouragement.

When we realize the complex world a man lives in, it is easy to understand why they become discouraged. If he is a young man, his future responsibilities may occasionally worry and discourage him. In his striving for acclaim, he may have lost, rather than won, some honor he has been striving for. Then his sensitive pride is always at stake. He is subject to insults, ridicule and the keen competition of his associates. He may be worried about money, or his family, or some special demands he cannot meet, or difficult problems he cannot seem to find solutions to. Or it may just be a bad day for him.

A woman has the power to break this spell of gloom, and the man 'senses this and turns to her for sympathetic understanding. A clever woman need not know the cause of his problems. She only needs to know the art of giving true sympathy. This art can be learned, by understanding a man's nature and just what it is he needs when he is discouraged.

How to Give True Sympathy

True sympathy means "sharing feelings." You are able to feel with him, or experience with him; even suffer with him. This understanding of feelings is a great comfort to him and seems to ease the pain. The way to do it is this: Come to him with warmth and friendliness and try to let him know that you understand just how he must feel. If he is very discouraged, tell him that "this is a dark hour that will pass." Try to maintain a pleasant attitude and whatever you do. Do not let his gloom rub off on you. Remember, one of the great powers of a woman is "to shed joy around and cast light upon dark days."

He wants you to feel with him, to lift his spirits with your spirit of hope and pleasantness.

If you find that you have not lifted the man's spirits, and then do not be discouraged. This does not mean that you have not been appreciated or helpful. Sometimes it takes a while for a man to "snap out of it," even though he has a sympathetic ear. He may need time and you will have to extend it to him. In the meantime, continue to show forth a sympathetic attitude.

Some Things Not to Do

Many women do not know the art of giving sympathy. It is not that they do not try but rather that they do not know how. They make all kinds of mistakes; say just the wrong things and often none of the right things. Their greatest mistake is that they try to help him solve his problems, offer too many suggestions, offer to help lift his burdens or remove his obstacles. These things may be appreciated, but they are not sympathy and not what a man needs from a woman. Practical help is not what he needs. He needs sympathy and the reassurance of your understanding and faith in him.

Also, do not make the mistake of minimizing his problems. Do not say, for example, "You worry too much," or "Your problems are just in your imagination," or "Life is not as tough as you think." These attitudes not only show a lack of sympathy but are belittling to his masculine pride. If you, a mere woman, can be so fearless in the face of difficulty, how can he feel like a man?

Also, it may not be wise to take the attitude of "count your blessings," for if you remind him that "he has two eyes, two hands and all the facilities to solve problems or make a success and he ought to be ashamed for letting life get him down," his worries will seem inexcusable. Not only will he feel a lack of sympathy from you, but he will be humiliated in your eyes. The fact that he has "blessings" can make his discouragement seem worse than ever, less justified. If he is reminded that in spite of his many blessings he has let life get him down, how can he possibly feel adequate as a man? Your lack of understanding sympathy, and your tendency to rob him of his masculinity will cause him to feel uncomfortable in your presence when he is discouraged. He will tend to avoid you in these moments of despair. You will have failed to give him one of the greatest gifts a woman can offer a man — an all comprehending sympathy. What the man wants is for you to understand his problem and sympathize with his feelings about it. Take the attitude, "Life is tough, how do you men put up with it?" and he will be encouraged to face life with a manly spirit.

Having a woman try to solve their difficult masculine problems only makes them feel ineffectual and incomplete as a man. This does not mean that she cannot offer suggestions when he asks for them. But when she gives advice it must be given in a feminine manner, as will be explained in the next characteristic. The main thing he seeks, however, is not her advice — no matter how great it may be. He seeks her comfort, solace and understanding when life is discouraging. And she can best mend his feelings by "shedding joy around and casting light upon dark days."

Chapter
8
The Role
of Man

Characteristic No. 6

His Desire to be Validated in His Role as a Man

Man was created by his very nature and temperament to play a certain part in life — a masculine part. It was intended from the beginning of time that he be a guide, protector and provider for his wife and children. Women were created for a different role — that of wife, mother and homemaker. The masculine and the feminine roles are complementary to each other. Neither one is more important than the other, but both are essential. Yet they are different from one another. In marriage, they have been compared to a lock and a key. They join together to form a perfectly functioning unit.

The important thing to remember about Characteristic No. 6 is this: Most men want to excel her in anything which requires masculine strength, skill, competence or ability. I would like to point out most emphatically that a man does not need to surpass a woman as a person, or to be more respected and honored than she.

77

Man the Leader

Because men were born to be leaders, they also inherited dominant masculine traits. Men are by nature more aggressive, forceful and determined than most women. Of course, there are exceptions to this rule. All the more reason for women to recognize the need for these hidden traits to come forward and help their man reach fulfillment as a male.

In the days of courtship, men have almost always taken the dominant position in their relationship with women, for they seek women out socially, ask them for dates and propose marriage. It works best when man is the pursuer — the woman the pursued.

Many girls, especially in our modem times, make mistakes in their relationships with men — mistakes that often drive men away. Many are too aggressive and thereby appear as a threat to the man's masculinity. We have all heard of the term "forward" in describing aggressive girls, but few know what it really means.

The Forward Girl

A girl who is forward has the following tendencies: She appears overly eager to win the attentions of men. By outrageous flirting, hints, suggestions or even directly asking, she indicates that she is definitely interested in the man and wishes that he would ask her out. She demonstrates an interest in him long before he has had a chance to even know if he is interested in her. She leads much too strongly. This is particularly true in the case of men who are very masculine and strong leader types. There might come a time when the man will want her to show an interest in him —to return the feeling that he has for her, but most men do not want her to be even more aggressive than he is.

Some other tendencies of the forward girl are to spend a lot of time talking about marriage, or how much she would like to have children, etc. These appear to a man as hints that the girl is serious about getting married, even when he is not. It could cause him to feel "on guard."

Of course, if the man brings up the subject of marriage or family life, it is all right to express your views. But other-wise, you are more interesting to men and more feminine if you avoid this subject before he is ready.

There are a few who make the mistake of being forward in affection, like grabbing him and kissing him, taking his hand, or putting her arm around him, etc. before he indicates any interest in her at all. Remember, most men like to be pursuers, the woman the pursued.

The rule is, never travel faster in love than he does. In romance the man leads and the girl follows. When he calls on you socially, do not rush to the door in uncontrolled exuberance! Hold your feelings in reserve until you are certain that he feels equally in love about you. And even then, do not express feelings greater than his own. This is not to suggest that you at any time appear unfriendly. But when you are friendly, do not single him out as one in whom you have special interest. Let him see that you are friendly with everyone you meet and that he is just one more man whom you happen to like very much and enjoy being with. Allow him the privilege of being the aggressor. When you do you help him to feel validated in his masculine role. As a result, he will be more apt to find you attractive and feminine.

Exceptions to the Rule

There is an exception to this rule and it is when the man is extremely shy or timid. He may be afraid of women or socially ill at ease around them and therefore does not play the part of the aggressive male. This does not mean that he does not have it deep in his nature, under some circumstances, to be the pursuer, but during the early stages of an acquaintance his inhibited nature might subdue these natural masculine traits. Young men are sometimes less confident around girls, but there are even some mature men that have never lost this disadvantage.

In the case of the shy man, whether young or old, a woman may, in the beginning of their romance, have to break some rules and show an overt interest in the man. He may have suffered lack of confidence around women and have the false notion that he is not attractive to them. The woman's interest, therefore, is an encouragement to him that he does have some traits that attract women.

A good example of a situation like this is in the movie "Goodbye, Mr. Chips." The leading man, Mr. Chips, was a schoolmaster who had had little experience with women. Although he was attracted to the young lady in the story, he was extremely reserved and shy. He did not know what love was all about, nor did he have the confidence to find out. The girl perceived that he did have a genuine interest in her and that his reserve was only due to his lack of confidence. She took an aggressive position, invited him to a dinner party, managed to get him alone and under the spell of a moonlight night hinted a proposal of marriage. She realized that unless she did something to bring him to romance he might shy away from it completely.

So, when a young woman is faced with the problem of under confidence in men, it is permissible to be more assertive, at least to some degree. But, as soon as she can, she should then retreat into her more feminine position and allow him to take the lead as long as she is still attracted to him.

One way to show respect for leadership is when the man turns to her for advice, as men often do. When men seek our opinions and wisdom, we should give it to them, but it is important that we offer them advice in the right way — a way that is feminine.

How to Give Feminine Advice

When you give advice or opinions, do so as a fountain that bubbles over in a park. Let him take as much or as little of your advice as he would like. Use no pressure or forcefulness. Have no unbendable opinions. Do not speak with such strong conviction that could cause him to feel obligated to take your advice or to be rude. Give him "take it or leave it" counsel. Use the words "I feel," or "I believe," for they are indicative of insight, which is a feminine gift. Remember the following don'ts:

1. Don't Appear to Know More Than He Does About a Subject He is Proficient In. This means that you should not map out a course for him to follow, analyze his problems or decisions or make a lot of suggestions.

2. Don't be Motherly. Avoid giving him the feeling that you are sorry for him and therefore would like to rescue him from his problems — protect him from the hard world.

3. Don't Talk Man to Man. When men give one another advice they "hash things over." Men are at times brutally honest and are apt to tear into the heart of a problem. They say such things as "Let's come to some conclusions," or "Why don't we go over it again," or "I think I know the big problem." When a woman takes this attitude, she appears as "one of the guys" and becomes less feminine. Remember, in giving a man advice stay as womanly as you can so that he will feel validated in his masculine role.

When you are in the presence of men who demonstrate the masculine traits of leadership, allow them the privilege of being the assertive male, and also express admiration for this masculine quality — at least occasionally. For example, if he is firm, has strong convictions on an issue, or if he makes decisions with fast and decisive judgment, don't miss the opportunity to say, "I notice that you make decisions with decisive judgment."

In your relationships with men, eliminate all signs of masculine aggressiveness, determination and unyielding opinions. This does not mean, however, that you should not be firm in your beliefs and in your moral convictions. It only means that when it comes to a man's position as a man, and as a leader, that you allow him to be the man and that you take the part of the feminine woman.

Man the Protector

Another part of the man's masculine role is that of being the protector. When we consider the man's body build and his brave capable character, it is apparent that one of his purposes in life is to be the protector for women and children. He is larger, has stronger muscles and greater physical endurance than women. Women are delicate and being smaller, aren't as strong. Women are like fine precision machines, created for the gentler tasks and which run smoothly and efficiently when used for the purpose intended.

In all periods of time women have needed protection from the dangers, strenuous work and the harshness of life. In the early history of most nations the very conditions under which people were forced to live made manly protection necessary. There were dangers everywhere. Wild beasts, snakes, chopping wood and building houses created situations which called for masculine ability. Protecting their loved ones, however, made men feel heroic and brave and an enjoyable sense of manliness.

Protection Today

The important thing today is that we let the man be a chivalrous male. We do not have as many physical dangers we had a generation ago, but we do still need masculine men. Many women are still afraid of spiders, mice, lightning, thunder and strange noises. We are also afraid of dangerous situations regarding crime, fire or abuse from others.

Women need to be protected from lifting heavy objects, moving furniture or anything which requires masculine strength and ability. On some occasions women need to be protected from offensive people who may make unreasonable demands. She turns to men in times of danger, strenuous work or in other difficulty.

Mistakes Women Make

Women today do not always turn to men for protection. In our generation, they have made the mistake of becoming much too independent; thinking they don't need men at all. We see them lifting heavy objects, repairing automobiles, changing tires, driving heavy equipment, fixing the roof, doing huge carpentry and many other masculine tasks. Day in and day out they are trying to prove that they do not need masculine care and protection, that they are well able to take care of themselves.

It is difficult to describe how often women rob men of their masculinity by acting as though men aren't needed. A competent woman stands as a threat to the male ego — and therefore to the romantic relationship we want.

When he comes in contact with a seemingly capable, efficient woman, one who acts as though she can meet him or defeat him on his own grounds, he does not feel like the man he longs to be. It is an unpleasant feeling that he might not care to repeat.

The woman also ground by becoming capable and independent. As she begins to take on this air of self-sufficiency, she risks losing some of her essential feminine charm. A feminine woman is tender, delicate and gentle and needs the protection of men. When we see a generation of women who act capable, beyond what they can achieve, it is not surprising to see that they have lost respect in the eyes of the men and that men do not offer them the chivalry that they did a generation ago.

The important thing to remember is this: Men enjoy protecting women. Do not think it is an imposition on a man to protect a feminine woman. The most pleasant sensation a real man can experience is his consciousness of the power to give his manly care and protection. Rob him of this sensation of strength and ability and you rob him of his feeling manliness. It can lessen his romantic feelings for you.

If you are going to observe Characteristic No. 6 — The Man's Desire to be Superior in His Role as Man — it will be essential to recognize his need to be a protector and to allow him this privilege. If you want to help your man to feel like your protector, you will take on the nature of a feminine woman. There are a number of things that you can do to make it easier for him to assume this masculine role, for example:

How to Let Him Be a Man

Take every opportunity to allow him to play the part of a chivalrous man. Let him open doors for you. If you are in a car, be sure to sit still until he comes around and helps you out. Be sure to always offer a gracious thank you. When he arrives to take you out socially, if you have a coat, hand it to him and turn your back so that he can help you with it. Young men can feel somewhat awkward in offering their chivalry, but we can help to make it easier by assuming it, and never shying away from their offers. Never lift a huge, heavy object in a man's presence. If he does not offer, ask him politely if he would please lift it for you. Men almost never mind. They enjoy helping women. Lean on them for everything that requires masculine help, strength, skill, ability or protection.

To prove the importance of helping a man feel masculine, let me tell you the following experience:

Romance Revived

A girl of my acquaintance was going with a young man that she liked very much, and they were getting quite serious about each other. Suddenly he stopped going with her for no understandable reason. She pondered the thought for quite some time, wondering what, if anything, she had done to drive him away.

About this time, she attended one of our Fascinating Girl classes and learned about the importance of not competing with men in masculine fields and was able to pinpoint her mistakes. She recalled that he had been bothered because she had been extremely competitive with him in math — a field that he had some pride in. She also recalled trying to outdo him in sports, and trying to impress him as an intellectual, hoping that he would be impressed with her above-average knowledge.

Instead, one day he said, "Janie, you are so smart it makes me sick." Shortly after completing the Fascinating Girl course, she chanced to meet him again, displaying a more feminine attitude. She was still good at math but didn't try to always beat him at it. He was friendly and asked her for a date. By this time, she knew just what to do and what not to say. They dated again frequently and one evening he said to her, "Janie, you are different than you used to be. I can't put my finger on just what it is, but you are different!" Well, she knew. She had dropped her very aggressive display of intellectual powers. She had stopped being competitive with him and it paid off, for they were soon married.

This does not mean that a woman needs to pretend to be less intelligent mentally. Men are attracted to highly intelligent women, but they do not appreciate someone who appears to be a "brain" or an "intellectual". Never compete with men in sports, or in the working world, or rival with them for some honor or contest or prize. Especially not a man you are in love with. In other words, do not try to out-do men in any of their fields of endeavor.

There are two main rules if you are to help a man feel masculine.

They are:

1. Need his masculine care and protection.

2. Do not compete with him in anything which requires masculine strength, ability or skill.

When you do these two things, you make a man feel like a man; you give him the wonderful feeling of validation in his masculine role.

Man the Provider

We now come to the role of the man as the provider — another part that he needs to play in his masculine role, and another part in which he needs to feel validated. Even when you are not married but dating, it is important to understand these principles.

Today, even though women everywhere are working, we still recognize the man as a primary provider, wherever possible. Most men know that when they marry they will assume this economic load for a wife and any possible children. A man's wife may or may not work, but it is not their direct worry, unless they are alone. He has a major responsibility here.

In understanding a man's position as the provider, let us refer again to Characteristic No. 6, the man's desire to be validated in his role as man.

Role as a Man

1. Admire his masculine strength and ability.

2. Do not show indifference or ridicule for his manly skills, strength or abilities.

3. With yourself: Don't be aggressive, or too efficient in masculine things.

4. Need his manly care and protection.

5. Do not try to excel him in anything which requires masculine strength.

6. Recognize him as a leader: In romance let him lead.

Summary of Understanding Men

We have learned that in order to become the kind of woman a man wants, the kind he can love and cherish, we must learn to understand men. We must know their characteristics, peculiarities and vulnerabilities and their basic needs and feelings, so that we will know just what to do and say in our associations with them. We will be able to avoid mistakes which drive men away, and instead learn the secrets which will help them to fall in love. The following are the basic characteristics we must understand:

Six Characteristics of Men

1. His need to be accepted at face value

2. His need for admiration

3. His sensitive pride

4. His secret reserve

5. His need for sympathetic understanding

6. His desire to be validated in his role as man

Woman's gift of understanding is one of the most moving forces which brings a man to her side and causes him to seek her constant company. She also fills a great need in his life as she becomes indispensable to his happiness and helps him grow as a man. The following experiences which were sent to me by letter, will illustrate:

How Understanding Helped a Young Man Grow

"I've been going out with this fellow for seven months and the change that's come over him is remarkable! When I first started going with him he was extremely reserved and self-conscious around everyone, especially me. He even blushed when he was spoken to. He also appeared as if he were half asleep or dull, with listless eyes. Our dates were spent in almost complete silence all the way there and back. I couldn't put up with this and I am sure he was also uncomfortable, so I started to exercise Fascinating Womanhood principles, especially admiring his manliness.

"Now he is alert and alive, has self-pride and a healthy male ego (not too much or not too little) and a good sense of humor. I didn't even know he was there before. He's really beginning to act like a man! He has a certain sparkle in his eye that appears as complete adoration every time he looks at me. Sometimes it is so strong that I can't meet his gaze. He is so considerate and always protecting me and watching out for me. He's always writing little poems and dedicating songs to me. He's so sweet and loving now. I love him!

"One night his final wall of reserve came tumbling down.

Maybe you would call it a Pandora's Box reaction, except the thoughts reserved were ones of gratitude and not past resentments. Here is what he said: 'You helped me stay happy through the hard times this year of hurting my leg and failing in my grades. You're always so happy. It radiates ... I feel I've grown up so much since I've met you... You've inspired me to break the school record in track and will inspire me to do it again in the fall. ... I get along with people so much better now... I don't know what I would have done this year without you. You're so cute when you get mad and bite your lip and open your eyes wide.' "Then when he was kissing me goodnight, with his voice full of emotion and tears, he passionately whispered, 'I love you,' and I believe him. I am so happy now, too, and I wouldn't be able to have all of this and more without the help of these principles of understanding men."

An Old Friend Returns

"After studying Fascinating Womanhood, I realized how many things were wrong in the way I related to men, so I began to practice the principles, which for a long time seemed so foreign to me, as I had lived such a self-centered life.

"Two weeks ago, I heard that an old boyfriend had been through a divorce and was coming to see me. I began to saturate myself with the teachings, made some feminine clothes and grew excited with the anticipation of seeing him again. Via letter I apologized for some of my mistakes when dating him 10 years ago and began to admire him. I told him I believed he had qualities of leadership which I had not recognized previously.

"When he arrived 5 days ago a miracle took place in me. The principles of Fascinating Womanhood became a natural part of me — not foreign anymore and I was able to be the kind of woman I wanted to be and the kind he wanted. As I accepted him, admired him and gave him his freedom to be himself I saw the most beautiful change begin to take place in him. I saw him become and reveal himself to be the kind of man I knew he wanted to be. He shed fears he had developed from his previous unsuccessful marriage. A new manly, domineering strength entered his life. "By the end of 5 days we had expressed love for each other and asked God to help us to know His will about our lives.

I feel like such a feminine woman and admire him as such a masculine man. This is the most wonderful experience I have ever been through."

Inner Happiness

In our study of the ideal woman, the kind a man wants and the kind he will love and treasure, we come to the second quality, that of inner happiness. Men just naturally seek the company of girls who are happy inside, as we all do. This inner beauty not only captivates the man's interest, but gives his spirits a lift, too, since happiness tends to be "catching."

As you will remember in the story of David Copperfield, Agnes shed such a peaceful influence upon David that it "soothed him into tears." Inner happiness is a quality of serenity, peace of mind and tranquility. Agnes possessed inner happiness for she had "a placid and sweet expression" and "tranquility about her, a quiet, good, calm spirit." A girl who has inner happiness is not necessarily free from problems, but she does have the power to face these problems, or disappointments or sorrows with a spiritual calm.

A girl who does not have inner happiness is easily upset, troubled, or even emotionally disturbed. She may be gloomy over small matters or discouraged with herself, or in turmoil about minor things. She cannot stand the stresses or strains of life, the disappointments or problems. When a man is in the presence of such a girl he may, if he has good character, be sympathetic towards her and even try to cheer her up but might not be attracted to her. Remember, one of the functions of a woman, as far as men are concerned, is to "shed joy around," and this is difficult if not impossible to do when one is not inwardly happy.

Inner happiness is a quality which must be earned. It cannot be "put on," as a smile. It is involuntary and comes as a result of a noble character. The blueprint for attaining this noble character will be explained in the next chapter. Do not be discouraged, therefore, if you are an unhappy person who is troubled or has suffered a lot in life. But regardless of what kind you have been through, you can build a wonderful character. You can become angelic and in so doing will automatically gain inner happiness.

The road to happiness, then, lies in the development of our spiritual side. It does not lie in any other direction, regardless of how many people may think otherwise. It is quite important to understand these "mistaken roads" to happiness, so that you will not be fooled or sidetracked into them.

Mistaken Roads to Happiness

Most of us are trying to be happy. It is one of the most central desires that each one of us has, and yet few people attain true happiness, which only proves that most people are pursuing it in the wrong direction.

The trouble lies in the fact that we seek happiness on a superficial road. We think that if we just had a charming wardrobe, or more beautiful hair, or a prettier face, then we would be happy. Or we may feel that if we could live in a particular community or had money for the comforts and pleasures of life, then we could be happy. Or we feel if we only had great friends or a loving family, then happiness would be easy.

These things do, of course, have value, but they are not the requirements for inner happiness. There are women who have none of these material things and a difficult life, yet they enjoy inner peace.

On the other hand, some who have them all are miserable. Some seek happiness by finding momentary pleasure.

The word pleasure comes from the word please. Pleasure is derived from those things which please the senses, such as the eyes, nose, ears, mouth and sensual feelings. There are both good and bad pleasures. The good pleasures are such things as sunshine, rain, flowers, the laughter of little children, music, wholesome recreation, spending time with loved ones or friends, the arts and many more of the finer things of life. There is pleasure in attractive clothes, a warm bubble bath, beautiful homes, gardens, furniture and the conveniences of modem equipment such as vacuum cleaners, washing machines, etc. These things are enriching to life, but we should realize that they bring pleasure rather than deep happiness. People who have all of the pleasures of earth, may yet fail to find happiness. Some pleasure does not bring happiness such as indulgences in immoral sex and selfish behaviors.

The Road to Inner Happiness

Happiness is quite different from pleasure. It arises from a different source. While pleasure arises from those things which please the senses, happiness may even come from unpleasant experiences, such as pain in childbirth, or going without sleep or even food in order to help someone in need.

Happiness comes from dedicated effort to fulfill our responsibilities in day to day living — no matter how great or small these duties may be. It comes from overcoming weaknesses and from reaching worthwhile goals and achievements. It is a result of losing our self-centeredness and becoming interested in the lives of others and developing a genuine love for them. Inner happiness is a direct result of the development of character. To review these sources of happiness:

1. Overcoming our weaknesses

2. Fulfilling our life's responsibilities

3. Losing our self-centeredness in our love for others

4. Reaching worthwhile goals or achievements

5. Developing a great character

Inner happiness is independent of others and outside circumstances. It is within the reach of each one of us through a dedicated effort in the right direction.

Women's Happiness

The way to happiness for a woman is the perfection of her angelic side. As she develops a kind, gentle, sympathetic character, yet one with strength of will, womanly courage and a sense of responsibility, she will grow towards this inner happiness essential to the ideal woman. Then, as she learns to understand men, she can attain the virtues of acceptance, understanding and appreciation, which further add to her happiness as well as the man she loves.

You may have heard the statement, "We are just about as happy as we make up our minds to be." Although there is some merit to this positive outlook, the statement is not entirely correct. A wicked person cannot acquire inner happiness through a positive attitude, nor can one who is living a selfish life. You cannot obtain inner happiness by determination alone. You must lay the proper groundwork by living true principles.

The Happy Woman

A girl who has inner happiness has an inner radiance to the eyes, a serene expression in the face. She has a lightness to her walk, a winsome manner that is inspired by the attitudes of optimism, faith and love. She smiles easily, is content, and is slow to criticize. She is trustful and patient, and her spirit radiates tranquility, serenity and peace.

Her appearance is uplifting to all who view her and fascinating to men.

In reaching the quality of inner happiness, I have said that it must be earned, and that it is earned by the development of a wonderful character. All of the virtues of character add to inner happiness, but there are two which I would like to mention as especially essential to women. They are the following:

Two Essential Virtues to a Woman's Happiness

Accepting ourselves: In the process of becoming Angels we are still human beings and therefore we will make mistakes.

1. Some of these errors can cause us to become quite upset with ourselves. Even little things could disturb us and rob us of happiness. It is not fair for us to be too hard on ourselves. If we can learn to be forgiving of others, we must do the same for ourselves. Just as we learn to accept men that we associate with, we must learn to accept ourselves as human beings and allow for our mistakes and weaknesses.

I read about a man who loved to travel the world over but was quite upset at times about a problem he faced in foreign lands. In some countries he was deliberately overcharged for purchases. These deceitful people took the joy out of his travels to a degree. By thinking about the problem, the man determined to set aside a certain amount of money for each trip "to be robbed of." From then on, he was able to enjoy his trip.

The businessman allows in advance for business failures. We should allow for mistakes as well. Tell yourself that each year, each week, and even each day you will make your share of mistakes or unwise decisions.

Accepting ourselves, however, does not mean contentment. It does not mean that we accept ourselves as foolish, unwise, weak or inferior human beings, making no effort to improve. This attitude would block our progress. It does mean that we accept ourselves as human, likely to make mistakes and use poor judgment at times, although we do make an effort to improve.

In our efforts to improve try not to become discouraged if old habits are difficult to break. In the swim upstream, we are occasionally pushed back by a wave or an opposing current.

2. Appreciation of the simple pleasures of life. Another virtue essential to happiness is an appreciation of the simple joys of life, such as visiting with a good friend, rain, sunlight, or fresh crisp curtains. It is not so much these simple pleasures themselves that contribute so much to a woman's happiness as it is her ability to appreciate them.

Little children have this ability to enjoy simple pleasures. An ice cream cone, a tub of water to splash in are common things they enjoy. The appreciative woman who learns to enjoy these common pleasures is never left wanting.

In summarizing the subject of inner happiness, be reminded of its essential value in feminine charm and that men especially are attracted to it. It is earned by the development of our angelic side, or our spiritual qualities.

Inner happiness is an upward climb. It is like swimming upstream and is found in the great efforts and achievements in life. It is earned by a personal victory over our weakness and an upward reach for the perfection of the spirit.

Chapter 10
An Admirable Character

In winning the interest of men we cannot overlook the importance of good character. It is, in fact, essential in becoming the kind of woman a man wants. Good men always either consciously or unconsciously look for traits of virtue in women.

Good character is the foundation of a charming personality in both men and women. If you will notice people who have "winning ways," you will observe that their charm is based upon traits of character. They are inclined to be kind, generous and considerate, with a genuine love and concern for others.

When a person loses the tendency to be self-centered, and develops a real interest in his associates, he can't help but win their friendship and respect. His good character has created for him a winning personality.

In a young woman, good character provides three things in winning the attention and interest of men. First, her worthy character provides the very basics for what most men are looking for in a woman. Then second, it is the framework of a winning personality. Her goodness, her kind consideration of others, her honesty and her strength of will are essential elements of her feminine charm. Then third, her good character will help her have a serenity in the face, a womanly beauty in her manner and her bearing that is especially appealing to men.

Contrast this with a girl who is selfish, deceitful and critical. She will have a personality that repels men rather than attracts them. As a result of her poor character she will not have the beauty of serenity but instead will have some hardness about the face. All of the expensive clothes and good grooming imaginable cannot counteract or hide her poor character.

Our Models for Study

Agnes, you will remember, had an angelic character. David Copperfield always associated her with a "stained-glass window in a church" and worshipped her from the time he first beheld her. Deruchette was known as the "living form of a benediction," and "sweetness and goodness reigned throughout her person." Amelia was "a tender little domestic goddess" whom men were inclined to worship. These girls must have had inspiring characters to have inspired such reverent feelings from the men in the stories.

And if you will refer to Chapter One in which I have described "true love," you will remember the worshipful love that John Alden had for Priscilla. "There is no land so sacred, no air so pure as the air she breathes, and the soil that is pressed by her footsteps." Also, the young woman that Victor Hugo loved inspired holy feelings in his heart for he writes: "If she only allow me to give my life to anticipating her every desire ... if she but permit me to kiss with respect her adored footprints."

These feelings of reverence could only be inspired by a woman of true worth and great character.

The Pedestal

A man wants a woman that he can "place on a pedestal" and worship her. Not only does he expect her to be good, but he wants to think of her as being better than he is. He would like to believe she is kinder, more patient and forgiving than he is. He rather considers himself to be the more unrefined creature of the human race. If he becomes thoughtless, harsh or critical he may believe it is common for men, but is disappointed to see a woman, the angelic creature of the earth, fall onto his level.

But before a man can place a woman on a pedestal she must develop a character that will lead to these feelings in him.

Dora was kind, honest and benevolent, but she did not earn the worshipful love of David Copperfield. There are many virtues of character, all worth every effort to acquire. The following, however, are ten of the most essential. Several are particularly important for young women.

Qualities of Character Essential to the Pedestal

1. Self-Mastery. "He who rules within himself and rules his passions, desires and fears, is more than a king." ~ Milton

Self-mastery is the foundation of a worthy character. We cannot even apply the knowledge which is in this book if we do not have the will to apply. Self-mastery in the highest sense means control over one's thoughts, feelings, desires, passions, fears and actions. It means deciding what is right or wise to do and then having the will to do it. It means sticking to a diet, controlling our words, dealing with our own feelings, keeping confidences or secrets that have been entrusted to us. It means being on time, fulfilling responsibilities assigned to us, holding to the standards that we set for ourselves and reaching our goals.

There are numerous ways of gaining self-mastery. Many philosophers have advised that we "do something difficult each day" to strengthen the will. Doing irksome tasks, demanding definite quotas of ourselves are some of the things that we can do to gain self-control, so that when problems come we will have fortified ourselves to endure them.

2. Unselfishness. Another mark of fine character is that of unselfishness. The dictionary describes selfishness as "caring unduly or supremely for oneself; regarding one's own comforts, advantages, etc., in disregard, or at the expense of that of others."

Some small children are by nature selfish. If you will notice, they can gather up every toy in sight and claim them for their own, without the slightest conscience for another child who may be crying at the top of his voice. But, as they are taught they learn unselfishness, learn the joy of sharing and giving. And as they grow towards maturity they hopefully lose this childish fault. Our growth towards becoming a finer person, in fact, is directly parallel with our ability to overcome egotism. Unfortunately, there are some who find it difficult to drop this trait and carry selfish tendencies throughout a lifetime. Young girls should take care lest they hang onto this childish fault of selfishness.

To be selfish is to live a narrow life. It is a real weak point of character. To be unselfish requires self-sacrifice. In fact, to give when there is no sacrifice would hardly be called unselfish.

For example, if you give away clothes that you dislike or do not need, it is not unselfish since there is no sacrifice. But if you give something of your own, which you like and want, but which you realize   someone else needs even more than you do, this is an act of unselfishness.

There is perhaps nothing which builds the angelic character of a woman more than unselfishness. It enlarges her spirit, enriches her life. Women such as this are blessings to this earth and in return they attain a beauty of spirit which is charming in their personality and which men admire greatly.

3. Love and Concern for Others. (Benevolence) Going a step beyond unselfishness is to have a genuine love and concern for others, especially those whom you associate with from day to day.

We live in a world of people who need our help in various ways. Some need physical assistance, but many more need only a word of encouragement or just the strength of a warm friendship.

One of the marks of a girl of fine character is her love and concern for her parents. Another mark of character is a concern for older people, for they are often desperately lonely and need the brightness of youth to cheer them.

I remember years ago knowing a young girl who was a friend to all of the elderly. She was charming and had many friends her own age, but she would always stop in church to converse to this or that older person, to laugh with them, pay attention to them and cheer them. Everyone loved her for her generosity.

The greatest enemy to love and character is a faultfinding attitude. It is impossible to love someone at the same time you feel resentful or critical towards him. The way to love is to accept a person as he is, both virtue and fault and then look to his or her better side and concentrate on that.

Those you bestow love upon will be quick to perceive it. They will be able to detect by the tone of your voice or the soft look in your eyes, your feeling of genuine love. But even without these outward expressions love is easily felt. It is the most wonderful feeling that human beings can experience and one that -people everywhere hunger for almost as much as they hunger for food. Giving true brotherly love is one of the greatest services that you can render.

4. Chastity. The word chastity specifically means "to not engage in sexual relations with anyone outside of marriage. This law of chastity is especially essential to the happiness of a woman, for a number of reasons.

There is a "new morality" which teaches an opposite doctrine. This not so new code teaches our youth that chastity is no longer important, that they can engage in "free love" with anyone, and that marriage is no longer important. It is strange that they think they can take a timeless principle, that has been tried and proven for thousands of years, and toss it out, thinking there will be no ill effects. One needs only to look around to see the results of this behavior.

In the first place, it does not lead to happiness. One of these laws is that you cannot be truly
happy unless you are morally clean. It is impossible, no matter how you may think otherwise.

For example, Dr. Max Levine, M.D. and Psychiatrist of New York Medical College said: "I speak not as a clergyman but as a psychiatrist. There cannot be emotional health in the absence of high moral standards and a sense of human and social responsibility."

It is highly foolish to give yourself to a man outside of marriage. Too many hearts have been broken, too many lives ruined when a girl yields without the protection of marriage. In other words, when a man is free to "help himself" to "love her and then abandon her" without the obligation of marriage, he may find it easy and desirable to do so.

Some girls foolishly think that they must yield to a man sexually because they may lose him if they don't. Actually, just the opposite is more likely to be true.

When a man can indulge himself in sex without the obligation of marriage, he is apt to take advantage of her and then walk away, free of the responsibility of marriage. She is more apt to lose than win.

There are, then, several convincing reasons for remaining chaste. First, we cannot have inner happiness without it. Second, strength of character is strengthened by being sexually pure. Third, considering the wise and foolish aspects, marriage is a protection to a woman, a protection she would be foolish to forfeit for the temporary pleasures of premarital sex.

5. Honesty. It is difficult to say which of the virtues are the most important, but honesty is certainly one of them. One cannot lead a moral and wholesome life if one is not honest. Most of us have been trained in the basics of honesty, in that we would not think or telling lies. These standards, however, do not necessarily make us an honest person, for we may be dishonest in the subtler forms.

Some of the more obscure forms of dishonesty are such things as cheating on tests, making excuses which are not entirely true, lying about our age, failing to return money or goods which do not belong to us, or which have been given to us by mistake, taking pay for jobs we did not complete, failure to leave identification for damaged property (cars, etc.), giving false reasons for improper conduct, failure to take the blame for bad behavior, etc.

In order to overcome these tendencies, it is important first to gain some moral courage. Then, one has to develop a sense of values, and be convinced that honesty is worth far more than material goods, comforts or our personal pride. To be honest in spite of any inconvenience or embarrassment to us will help us to gain character and inner happiness.

Another form of honesty is sincerity. Men in particular appreciate this quality in women. A man admires a woman who is at all times herself, who does not put on the false front of trying to be someone else. There are some girls who make the mistake of being one thing at home and trying to be quite another when they are out socially with men.

Whatever your true personality, try to discover it, polish it up so that it will be at its best and then give it to the world without apology.

6. Humility. Humility is an honest estimation of ourselves as we really are, and as God sees us. It is not low self-esteem. It means viewing ourselves not less than we are, or more than we are, but just as we are. It means an evaluation of our good points and recognizing our weaknesses. It does not mean "groveling" or denouncing ourselves as inferior human beings. It is an honest evaluation.

True humility is one of the most essential elements of a noble character. All truly great people in this life have had humility, regardless of their position or outstanding qualities. They have been able to see themselves in a true light, have been able to recognize their greatness and yet have acknowledged their weaknesses. No one is so great or good that he has no need of humility.

When we are tempted to be critical of someone, we can keep ourselves humble by remembering our own faults and imperfections.

True humility brings with it the qualities of patience, forgiveness, acceptance and love. It is almost impossible to love someone without humility. In our striving for a worthy character and climbing to the position of the pedestal, we should not lose our spirit of humility or we will lose one of the foundation stones of character.

7. Moral Courage. Moral courage is the ability to live according to our own healthy convictions. It means a firmness or

determination to live that which we believe with a disregard for the pressures of others to persuade us to live otherwise. It is one thing to set standards for ourselves and quite another to have the moral courage to be true to these standards.

For example, you may determine to get good grades this semester but find it difficult to study all that is necessary.

8. Forgiveness. To forgive is to be willing to pardon a wrong that someone has committed against us.
For example, when someone has been critical, has said some unkind things about you behind your back, the tendency is to become resentful of that person.

Forgiveness is a higher law — one that goes beyond justice. Since this higher law runs counter to human nature it requires effort and self-discipline to live it and to overcome the tendency to become resentful. The best way to learn forgiveness is to remind yourself of your own faults and weaknesses. This will make you much more patient and forgiving of others.

People of good character and personality have learned to forgive. They are able to rise above the trivial things in life and concentrate upon the good and the beautiful in others. Admirable and angelic women have always had this quality.

The important thing to keep in mind is that forgiveness is essential to a noble character — one worthy of a pedestal and attractive womanhood. If you want to be the kind of a woman that the man you love worships, you will want to learn to forgive others and not hold grudges. Their actions and weaknesses are not your responsibility. Your responsibility is only to forgive them.

9. Self-Dignity. Those who have self-dignity have a proper respect for themselves, never place themselves in an inferior position, nor will they allow others to reduce them to an inferior position. They have a stability of spirit, a feeling of self-worth which keeps them from being treated as an inferior.
Those who lack self-dignity tend to be too willing to please. In an effort to win friendship of another person, they do many special favors.

People of all ages make this mistake. College students, for example, sometimes loan cars and clothes to those they want to impress, in an effort to win their favor. An unpopular boy may loan his car to a boy he considers socially respected; a shy girl may loan her clothes to a girl she considers better looking and more popular; or she may offer to wash her dishes, sew her clothes or cater to other requests in an unconscious effort to gain her friendship. Sadly enough, instead of winning favor they are more apt to be further spurned for their lack of self-respect.

Another sign of lack of self-dignity is the tendency to be easily pushed around, walked on or abused. It is not in our nature to respect those who can be trampled on. Men do not respect women who will allow this mistreatment. They admire women who have some spunk and enough self-dignity to defend themselves. A later chapter will deal with this special problem and will outline just the right way to handle these situations in a way that will preserve self-dignity and charm and at the same time add to her relationship with a man.

Still another evidence of lack of self-dignity is in placing oneself in the position of pleading or begging, since it reduces one to an inferior position. Self-dignity implies a "queenly attitude and bearing" and is a matter of character as well as charm.

It in no way indicates a lack of humility but rather shows a proper respect for self, as we would for any other of God's creatures.

10. Gentle, Tender Quality. A quality of character especially important for women is gentleness. It is the framework upon which we build true femininity. Charming women of fine character have gentleness in abundance, without reservation. This does not indicate weakness or a lack of moral fiber or firmness. Gentleness is a part of the feminine nature — and essential to womanly character.

The quality of gentleness is a combination of several other virtues such as sympathy, benevolence, understanding, compassion, long suffering and kindness. These qualities combine to form the gentle, tender quality we speak of here.

If there is anything which will destroy feminine charm and along with it the illusion of an angelic character, it is a fierce frown, a hard expression about the mouth or a bitter tone in the voice. These outer expressions indicate a hard-unyielding character and one which is not represented in our ideal of an angelic woman.

The women that we all admire, both men and women alike and especially little children, are those wonderful angelic creatures who are soft spoken, who have firm but gentle attitudes, quick to forgive our offenses, slow to criticize us for our mistakes, who lend to the household an atmosphere of peace and harmony due to their gentle natures.

These are the angels men speak of in their memoirs. Usually these same men admit that they did little to deserve the kind, gentle understanding of such a mother or a wife, but they appreciate her all the more because she gave them more than they deserved.

Gentleness is, in fact, a part of real character when it is habitual, when we try every moment of the day with every person we meet.

How to Acquire a Beautiful Character

There are many other virtues of character. These are only 10 of the most essential. You can acquire a beautiful character in the same way that you would acquire any other accomplishment, by diligent effort.

Since there are many virtues worth attaining, it will be best to take them one at a time. Decide which is your weakest point and then work on that for a month or two, or as long as is necessary to make some real progress. Then go on to another and another, and back again to your weaker ones. You don't have to be perfect.

Be Sincere and Consistent

Do not think that you can be successful if you merely pretend to have good character. Insincerity is a form of dishonesty and many will see through it. If you are to win the interest of good men your character will have to be genuine. If you insist upon keeping a skeleton in your closet it is bound to rattle around occasionally and betray your insincerity.

If you are to be successful, you will also have to be consistent. You cannot appear be angelic on some occasions and immature on others.

Once you begin to improve your lovely character you will want to try to stick to it all the time. There may be times, being human, when you will slip back into old undesirable habits, but this is normal. If you continually strive for a fine character, progress will be certain.

Let Your Light Shine

There are different ways of "letting your light shine." If you acquire the nine traits of character mentioned here men will perceive your character by the angelic "light" which radiates from your face. However, they will not be altogether convinced of your true worth until they see your true character in action.

The following are some methods of "letting your light shine":

How to Let Your Light Shine

1. Hold to Your Ideals. If you will hold to your high standards and ideals, in your normal experiences with men you will have many occasions which will reveal your angelic side. These will come without any conscious effort on your part. The man you love will gradually come to know your true worth.

2. Appreciate His Character. Another method of proving your own worth is to appreciate his. If you appreciate him only because he looks polished and well groomed, or because he is a lot of fun, you do only a little to show your character. But if you appreciate him because he is honest, dependable and fair, you show him that these attributes are important to you.

3. Appreciate the Character in Others. Your estimation of others is a real indication of your own character. For example, if you are faultfinding and harsh in your judgment of your friends, you give yourself away as a person of superficial character, perhaps lacking the qualities of forgiveness, patience and humility.

But if you recognize and treasure unselfishness in others, or benevolence and patience, etc., then you show that you have a character that appreciates these qualities.

Shaking the Pedestal

As I have stated in the beginning of this chapter, when a man considers the ideals of womanly character he likes to think of her as being better than himself and therefore.

Now in man's relationship with women he tends to shake the pedestal at times or test her character. He wants to see for himself if she is as angelic as she appears to be, to see if she will hold fast to her position he has put her on.

He may not be aware he is even shaking the pedestal, but consciously or unconsciously he wants to find out for himself her true worth.

In testing her he may, for example, suggest that she lower her standards or deviate in some way from her true character. If she remains true to her ideals, his admiration for her is reaffirmed. Remaining on the pedestal is only further proof that she belongs there. If, however, she lowers her standards and falls from the pedestal to a lower level, he is naturally disappointed in her.

We women must realize the seriousness of a man's attempt to shake the pedestal or to test our character. If we fall, not only do we injure ourselves, but we lose respect in the eyes of the man we love.

An impressive example of pedestal shaking is found in the novel The Portrait of Dorian Gray.

The girl in the story was a moral girl. She loved Dorian Gray and they were engaged to be married. Just prior to their proposed marriage he tempted her by asking her to engage in pre-marital relations with him.

At first, she was shocked; then disappointed, she turned to walk away. As she reached the door she hesitated, thought about it, and an immense fear seized her, a fear that she may lose him if she refused. She turned around and came back to him and yielded to his request. The next day Dorian Gray expressed his great disappointment in her and his reluctance to marry her.

He shook the pedestal, but she fell off. The poor girl, brokenhearted and rejected, committed suicide. Of course, in this story, Dorian Gray was a wicked man and the girl was fortunate she didn't end up with him. However, if she had not yielded to him, she would not have died but would also have preserved her dignity and her self-esteem.

Conclusions

A man can deeply love a woman of angelic character, one he can place on a pedestal and one who can inspire a feeling of adoration in his heart.

If you acquire a fine character and meet the test, you will have one of the essential elements of Angela Human, the kind of girl a man adores.

The Domestic Goddess

The fourth quality of Angela Human is her domestic or homemaking ability. This means that she must be able to cook, manage a household, care for children, handle money wisely and a myriad of other things that go to make up a great homemaker. These qualities are only a small part of the ideal woman, but they are essential.

Domestic qualities are found in our studies of Agnes, Amelia and Deruchette. Agnes was "as staid and discreet a housekeeper as the old house could have." Amelia was a "kind, smiling, tender little domestic goddess whom men are inclined to worship." Deruchette's "presence lights the home" and "her occupation is only to live her daily life." Then the author says, "When womanhood dawns, this angel flies away; but sometimes returns, bringing back a little one to mother."

These three girls, who represent at least in part our ideal of Angela Human, had qualities of the domestic goddess — qualities that men notice and admire in women.

What Men Want

It is important that you understand just what it is men want in women, in different stages of their relationship. When a man first becomes acquainted with a girl, for example, he is not particularly interested in her ability to cook or sew. Her ability to be good company is far more important at this stage.

But later on, if he becomes interested in marrying her, he will begin to look more deeply. He will begin to notice her ability to cook well, her neatness and orderliness, her ability to handle money wisely, etc. It is an advantage if a girl can have a good knowledge of these subjects, but if not, she should at least have an interest and a willingness to learn.

A good man wants a girl who has a true sense of values, who counts love and daily fun as important as a clean house and good meals. He hopes to find a girl who can make a house a home.

There are some women who think only of the mechanistic part of homemaking, are too concerned about only basic cleaning and not enough about the atmosphere of a home. Their home becomes an empty shell and, although they may have polished floors, clean sheets and cupboards, they are not fascinating homemakers for they have ignored the very heart of the home — love, understanding and kindness. After all, the only thing that counts in life is people and the home should serve only the purpose of making a family comfortable and happy and serving both their material and spiritual needs. The men you know may have observed this emptiness in some homes and may have definite ideas about its tremendous lack.

They may not want to take a chance of repeating it in their home of their future.

A man does not want a girl who advertises her domestic interests in an effort to gain his affection. For example, she may say, "I can't wait until I have children," or "marriage is the main thing I want in life."

Although these are indications of your domestic interests, your efforts to "sell yourself" cause you to appear to be man hunting. This is not attractive.

This is especially bad early in your acquaintance before he has had a chance to get to know you or to appreciate your charming qualities.

Most men are attracted to girls who know more about the feminine arts than he does. He does not appreciate it if she asks him questions such as "What kind of tomatoes should I buy?" or "which fabric is better?" He probably won't want to provide the answers to women's problems. To do so makes you appear unqualified in your own field and gives him the impression that he knows more about it than you do. Just as we expect men to be more capable in the masculine things, more qualified as leaders, protectors and providers, men expect women to excel them in the feminine arts.

A woman is more interesting if she is somewhat of a mystery and keeps some of her qualifications to herself. She should reveal only a small part of that which she knows and subtly indicate that she has a whole store of knowledge yet to come which he knows nothing about.

In this way he will detect that there is more than appears on the surface, that there are hidden qualities that will be intriguing for him to discover. A woman of mystery is much more interesting to many men than the woman who tells all.

If you want to be a domestic goddess, prepare early and learn some basic homemaking skills. Do not wait until you are married to begin learning to cook and keep the house clean. When you become proficient so that when the right man comes along they will be second nature to you. You can go beyond the call of duty and become a "domestic goddess."

The following are suggestions to get you started in the right direction.

How to Be a Domestic Goddess

To be a Domestic Goddess you have to go beyond the mere call of duty and do your jobs well. If you give the bare stint of requirement, merely feed and clothe your family and sweep and dust or do a half- hearted job of cooking and homemaking, you will not be a feminine Domestic Goddess. The woman who succeeds is the one who really makes something of her responsibilities. She adds a kind of glory to her work that sets her apart as a goddess, and this glory comes primarily from doing her work well.

Besides this, a Domestic Goddess adds some feminine touches to her duties. Typical of her might be doilies, soft curtains and pillows, and in cooking she includes foods which have delicious aromas.

We can enjoy domestic tasks, doing dishes, scrubbing floors, etc. There is great satisfaction in doing anything well.

In summary we can say that a Domestic Goddess has principally three main qualifications. She:

1. She does her essential homemaking tasks well so therefore has satisfaction in it.

2. She adds feminine touches.

The following are some general suggestions to help you get started in doing your home duties well and also in adding some feminine touches. These might be slightly different before you are married if you are still living at home:

Homemaking

The following will result in greater efficiency in homemaking:

1. Concentration. The management of a household requires at least some concentration. Some women can't daydream and ponder problems and at the same time expect duties will be performed with efficiency.

There are specific tasks, like ironing, cleaning windows and washing dishes in which a wandering mind possible, but most of our tasks, especially any amount of tidying or organizing, requires thought as well as hands. So, put other thoughts out of your mind and concentrate on getting the job at hand done and out of the way.

2. Organization. Basic good homemaking depends upon being organized. This means having a place for everything and some

type of plan or to follow. I know that women dislike schedules, but lack of planning can lead to disorder. Men very much appreciate a well-organized household, where home life runs smoothly and without confusion.

3. First Things First. Also important is the habit of putting first things first. This means to concentrate on the more essential tasks while placing as secondary those things of lesser importance. If you will list your six most important homemaking responsibilities and then arrange them in order of importance, then use it as a guide each day, it will increase your efficiency, for example:

1. Appearance

2. Washing and ironing

3. Meals

4. Imperative shopping

5. Neat house

6. Auxiliary things

Although young women will not have the full responsibility of a household yet, sometimes they share this responsibility. Learning how to manage their portion of homemaking while still unmarried will help them to assume this responsibility later.

4. Simplicity. It will help to simplify life and get rid of excess clutter if you are to excel as a homemaker. Clean out your closets and drawers and live simply. This makes domestic chores easier and more enjoyable.

5. Work. Nothing worthwhile in life is easy and it certainly is not easy to be a good homemaker. You can expect it to be work, but you can also expect that it will pay rich dividends. Work is good healthy self-esteem both physically, mentally and spiritually, to say nothing of the comfort and pleasure it brings to you and the family who lives in a clean well-ordered home.

These are the five essentials of good homemaking:

1. Be Genuine. As a girl goes out into the world she is usually wise enough to represent herself as a clean and tidy girl. She is careful to have washed hair and clothes, etc.

Some girls, however, are quite another thing at home. They may have dirty bedrooms, messy closets and drawers and unclean habits. Be genuine and consistent. You will not only present a clean image in public, but you will actually be that image in your own home.

2. The Feminine Touch. In addition to a clean, well-organized home, the Domestic Goddess provides some feminine touches to housekeeping. Things like soft pillows, frilly curtains, and bowls of fruit, doilies, gingham curtains, soft rugs, artistic pictures and ornaments reveal a feminine touch.

3. Sewing. Girls of today are fortunate in that there are so many fine classes in sewing. They learn the most effective techniques and shortcuts to making a garment look really professional. Even you just learn enough about sewing to mend or alter clothing, which can be very helpful.

I remember noticing while in a public gathering an extremely attractive girl with a striking dress on. I felt at first glance that her dress had certainly been purchased at an exclusive dress shop and that she paid a high price for it. But on closer scrutiny, I noticed that her zipper was not exactly straight, and that there were other signs that it was handmade.

This did not detract from the effect, however. She was stunning, dress and all. It was quite convincing to me that if you design a dress that is as special as this one was, the construction will somehow pass.

I wish to stress that it is important for girls to learn to sew if they are able to. There are occasions all during her lifetime when sewing will be of real value. Being able to hem or sew on a button at least is key. Emergencies can arise when sewing is a real answer to problems.

4. Cooking. Men are inclined to put cooking at the top of the list of domestic arts. They love good food, well prepared. It is important to learn to cook a number of dishes and menus that many men like.

If you want to add great touches to your cooking, include foods which smell delicious. Things like onions frying, homemade bread, cinnamon rolls, etc., arouse sentiment and appreciation. These things set a woman apart as a domestic goddess.

5. Handling Money. Another gift of the domestic goddess is to know how to handle money. After marriage she will need to do much of the buying, especially for the household. She will have to learn to "make a dollar stretch." Men tend to notice a girl's tendencies to be extravagant or wise with money. One of the man's greatest fears in taking the step of marriage is the fear of

financial responsibility. A woman who is extravagant could propose a real problem in the future. Thrift is a virtue in women, and one that we should cultivate in our youth. Here are a few ideas to follow:

If you are making money or have an income, after you deduct your basic monthly expenses, try to save at least half of what you make. This seems simple and easy, but actually it requires considerable self-discipline to follow this rule. There will be many temptations to buy things which you do not need.

Another rule is to buy or make good clothes and then take care of them so that they will wear as long as possible.

Keep clothes clean and mended. They wear better this way. The economy wardrobe includes some clothes that are plain and basic, that tired of everything else. You can change their appearance by a change of scarf, necklace, a different collar, etc. Some basic plain skirts are also economical and can be coordinated with many different tops.

Don't be hasty in your buying. If you definitely know what you want, buy it. But if you are at all uncertain, and if the item costs at least $20.00 or more, it is safer to go home and think about it. The next day if you still want it buy it. Here again, this is not as easy as it sounds. There will always be the temptation to "buy it now" and save time. You will save more money, however, if you make this a rule in your buying. Don't buy anything which is not what you really want.

Beware of letting money slip through your fingers on small items which you think you need.

Motherhood

Part of the domestic role is motherhood. To be a wonderful mother is one of the most important contributions that a woman can make to our society. Do not think that leaving the home and centering your life around a career, making some notable contribution to the world there, can compare to the success of rearing a family. You can inspire them to high standards and goals, helping them to grow both physically and spiritually, giving them love and sympathy in times of trouble and finally, helping them to take their place in the world.

On the other hand, deserting your position as a mother, and as a result causing your whole family to fail to reach their potential, or even fail as individuals, is a big mistake.

This is not to say that a woman cannot be successful as a mother and still have a career, but it will be very difficult.

Our most sacred responsibility is to be a successful mother and to rear to maturity the precious souls God has given us and to do the best job of mothering that we possibly can. If we do, we can have, in peace of mind.

Not only is it our sacred responsibility to rear children, and to do it wholeheartedly, but we must realize that men admire this dedication in women. A good man will notice and admire a woman who loves little children, and who wants children of her own. The idea of the Domestic Goddess is not only to be a mother, but to have an abundant willingness to do so and to be the most wonderful mother possible.

Method of Becoming a Domestic Goddess

1. Do your tasks well.

2. Add some feminine touches.

3. Be happy in your domestic duties.

We have also learned just how to enjoy homemaking, so that we will be happy. We have learned that we should have a proper attitude about work, to face it realistically for just what it is — part enjoyable and part drudgery. Our happiness comes in the overall accomplishment. We have also learned that if we are to enjoy working, we will have to allow enough time to enjoy it, and this means not allowing ourselves to be too crowded for time, whenever possible — or eliminating non-essentials that waste our time. And last, if we are to enjoy our homemaking we will have to do a second mile job — or go beyond the call of duty.

How to Find Joy in Tasks

1. Proper attitude towards drudgery.

2. Allow time to enjoy homemaking.

3. Do your jobs well.

If you will give thought to this subject and apply reasonable effort even though your social life and education are more important at this stage, you will form habits that will be valuable to you later on, when you are married. You will be on your way to being a Domestic Goddess.

A Matter of Character

You may never have thought of this before, but good homemaking is a matter of character since it requires thoughtfulness, unselfishness, and consideration of the feelings of others, organization, diligence, understanding, patience, kindness, forgiveness and almost every virtue in existence. A woman has a most wonderful opportunity right in her own home to develop her character by being a wonderful homemaker.

Beyond the Domestic Goddess

Remember that although the idea of the Domestic Goddess is essential to our picture of the ideal woman, a man wants more than just a homemaker. He wants a recreational partner and an intellectual companion. He also hopes she has a broad interest in life and all that is in it — its many problems, its many faces and its wondrous beauty.

The ideal woman needs to be a part of the world outside the home, needs to feel a certain debt to society — a sense of social responsibility.

We now come to the end of our study of the Angelic qualities, the side of our ideal woman that awakens in a man a feeling of near worship and the side that brings him true happiness. But we have to realize that although these qualities are essential to him and to his true love for a woman, a man hopes for more than an angel. He also wants a woman who is human.

The Human Side

The human side of our ideal woman is composed of a myriad of charming and fascinating qualities. It is her girlishness, her dependency upon man, her delicacy and her femininity. It is also her joyfulness, vivacity and her teasing playfulness.

Add to all this a rosy glow of vibrant health and a dash of spunk and sauciness and an underlying attitude of trust and tenderness and you begin to build a delightfully human creature, one that will win a man's heart.

The human qualities fascinate men. They enchant him, captivate him, amuse him and also arouse in him a tender feeling — a desire to protect and shelter. They set off a spark, or a driving force in a man that can cause him to do what appears almost to be a foolish thing. This is the mad adoration and indulgence that can lead him to a pinnacle of joy or destruction.

The Human qualities, in some instances, might cause a man of intelligence and character to marry a girl of who only seeks to use him. One would expect such a man to choose a more sensible companion, but her Human appeal has made love blind. The fascination David Copperfield had for Dora was due to her Human characteristics and caused him to turn from the angelic Agnes to marry Dora. The Human qualities have tremendous power. They have more immediate influence over most men than the Angelic.

They are not difficult to acquire; they are not foreign to your nature, for they are woman's natural instincts. If you do not have them, it is because they have been suppressed. They enrich a man's life and when combined with the Angelic cause a man to experience celestial love.

Chapter 12
Femininity

Femininity is a gentle, tender quality found in a woman's appearance, manner, actions and her general attitude. No other quality has so much appeal to men, for it is such a direct contrast to his own strong and firm masculinity. This contrast, when brought to his attention, causes him to feel manly and this realization of his masculinity is one of the most enjoyable sensations he can experience. The extremely feminine woman is charming to men. The woman who is completely lacking in it may even be repulsive to men.

Femininity is acquired by accentuating the differences between yourself and men, not the similarities. You apply this principle in your appearance, your manner and your actions and even your attitude. The more different you appear from men the more feminine you become.

1. Feminine Appearance. To be most fascinating to men, women should wear only those styles and fabrics which are the least suggestive of those used by the men and which therefore make the greatest contrast to men's apparel. Masculine men never wear anything fluffy, lacy, gauzy or elaborate.

2. Materials. Avoid such fabric as tweeds, herringbones, hard finish woolens, denims, glen plaids, faint dark plaids, pin stripes, shepherd checks and geometries, since these are materials that men wear.

3. The Exception. The above materials can be used, if distinguished by an extremely feminine style or color. That way, the woman displays the stark difference between her and a man all in one ensemble. Otherwise they can give no help in making men realize how womanly you are! You will bring out the contrast between your nature and his.

Do wear soft woolens, soft or crisp cottons, soft and drapery synthetics, floral prints, polka-dots, animated designs, etc. The extremes of femininity are such things as chiffon, silk, lace, velvet, satin, fur, angora and organdie. Every woman should include as many of these in her wardrobe as she can afford and find appropriate to wear. These should be worn when trying to make the most feminine appeal to men.

Colors which are extremely feminine are pastels and vivid colors since men generally do not usually wear them, especially in Western cultures. Those colors to avoid are the drab and dull colors used by men, such as browns, grays, deep blue and charcoal.

These colors may be used effectively, however, if they are cut in an extremely feminine style, or trimmed with soft or bright accessories.

Therefore, use extreme care in selecting a print, to make sure that it is a pretty design and does not dominate you.

4. Style. Avoid tailored styles or any suggestion of masculinity such as buttoned cuffs, lapels, and top stitching unless combined with something deliberately feminine.

Extreme feminine styles are such things as full skirts, ruffles, scallops, puffs, gathers, drapes, flowing trains and many others. These styles are not always in fashion, nor are they appropriate for every use. Do use them whenever you can, and if they are becoming to you. There are feminine styles that are always available which can be used for any occasion.

The Victorian dress is feminine, for example, and conservative enough for most occasions. The gown itself, for that matter, is feminine, for men do not wear them. It is difficult to advise a feminine style which would be suitable for all women since we vary in figure and taste. A safe rule is to remember to accentuate the difference between you and men and to avoid any style which has a strong suggestion of masculinity unless softened in some way by a feminine effect.

Should women wear pants? Young girls are in so many sports and activities that the custom for them to wear pants seems to be universal and men have accepted the idea. When you do wear pants, soften the effect by color, material or accessory. You may want to wear a ribbon or headband in your hair, for example, or a scarf at your neck. The most feminine pants, for special occasions, are made of fabrics like white lace, black satin, brocade, etc. They can be beautiful and extremely feminine.

Back to dresses, trim can give a feminine effect to an otherwise plain dress. Lace, ribbons, colorful tie, fringe, embroidery, beads and braids can accentuate femininity.

5. Accessories. Avoid purses which resemble men's brief cases and shoes of masculine style. Wear soft scarves, flowers, jewelry and hair ornaments. In achieving a feminine appearance, the important thing to remember is the over-all impression which you make. Work for softness, airiness, delicacy and striking contrast to masculinity. The effect can be fascinating to men. The following two examples will illustrate:

How to Turn Men's Heads

I remember hearing of a pretty girl who bought a complete outfit in brown tweed for street wear — brown shoes, tailored brown coat with a brown fur collar and a stark brown hat. It was perfect in style, in taste and in fit and her women friends admired it immensely. But as she went along the crowded street she attracted no attention from men.

A little later she purchased a light blue coat, smart in style and vivid in color. To complete the outfit, she added light grey shoes and little blue hat, with touches of pink and blue. Neither, in her own opinion nor in the opinion of her friends was the outfit as tasteful or as harmonious as was the brown outfit. She was considerably surprised, therefore, when she wore the second outfit, to discover when she passed along the same crowded street that not a man would pass without an interested glance in her direction. With the brown outfit, she could get on the city bus without a man offering her a seat, but with the vivid blue and grey outfit, one man after another, somehow, always felt compelled to sacrifice his comfort for her sake. She was considerably surprised to watch the great difference the change of outfits made with the men. The explanation however, is very simple.

The first outfit was too much like what the men themselves wear, in color, in style and in this case, even material. It could not be expected to make her appear as a feminine woman. The second outfit, on the contrary, consisted of combining colors and style that most men would ever dream of wearing. Naturally this outfit helped to emphasize the fact that here was a woman, as different from men as could be, a girlish girl, the essence of femininity, the kind of woman a man likes to protect and cherish. Men are interested in women who give such an impression in her outward appearance.

Another incident involved a young girl who went weekly to a local market, dressed in ordinary clothes. She was not poorly dressed, but neither was she dressed in any way that would attract the attention of men. One day, however, she bought a beautiful dress of rich and beautiful colors in a gorgeous design. The dress was straight and to the ankles, of rich purple and deep pink, combined in a lovely artistic and large pattern. She wore her long black hair loosely down her back and a pink ribbon in her hair. When she went to the local market, on this single trip three different male employees stopped her and asked her if she would like to work at the market. They said they would recommend her as a cashier. She couldn't help but be amused that she had been in the market dozens of times before and not a single man had noticed her or stopped to talk to her — to say nothing of offering her a job.

Good grooming: Another part of the feminine appearance is to be well groomed. We need not dwell on this since there is much emphasis on grooming today anyway. We need only mention that clean, well-groomed hair, clean body and clothes are essential to the feminine appearance.

In bringing out the charming contrast between yourself and men, you must have an all-absorbing pride in your appearance. You must endeavor to be at your best every minute of the day.

Modesty

Still another part of the feminine appearance is modesty. In spite of the emphasis in our times on the "sex symbol," good men do not respect women who expose too much of their bodies to the public. Not only should the body be reasonably covered but also the underwear. Many men dislike hanging slips, bra straps that show and exposed underwear when a girl sits on a chair.

Girl-Watchers

I would like to include in this section an article which was printed in a San Diego newspaper about a group of young boys in a San Diego Junior High School, who formed a club called "Girl-Watchers." Here is what the newspaper had to say about them and their views on femininity:

"There is a 'Girl-Watchers' club at the Lakeside Junior High School in San Diego. It has a membership of 39 boys. Near the close of the last semester of school, the club published and distributed to all girls on the campus the following proclamation:

"We, the boys of Girl-Watchers Club, have been watching girls for the past four weeks. Some of what we have observed has pleased us. BUT, much of what we have seen displeased, disgusted and repulsed us. Therefore, we have agreed and resolved that some changes must be made. We feel the changes suggested are reasonable and fair. In general, all we are asking is that girls again become feminine in their thoughts, words and deeds because they should be different from boys.

"We are tired of constantly being forced to look at girls' underwear. For example: slips hanging out; skirts not long enough to cover underwear during such normal activities as sitting, stooping, reaching up or running. Boys do not like the carelessness girls display when sitting with legs apart or lying on floors, grass, benches and retaining walls, constantly making others look at their underwear. This is no thrill for boys or anyone else — just obnoxious!

"We are disturbed by girls who wear improper hose. Too many are wearing hose not long enough. The viewer is greeted by the unlovely sight of hose tops, garters and bulging thighs all hanging below skirts. Ugh!

"We find girls draped in boys' or men's clothing unattractive and unfeminine. Many are wearing sailors' pea-jackets, boys' shirts with tails hanging out ... and sundry other items of male clothing. Wear your own clothes and let us wear ours.

"We have been frightened too many times by girls who use makeup with little or no skill or even good sense. It is hideous! Use a little makeup; learn how to apply it.

"We are concerned about girls' choice of vocabulary in both spoken and written communication. We take a dim view of girls using both profane and obscene language in their conversation with each other and with us. Clean up your mouths or keep quiet. We think girls' passing notes around is silly but girls passing obscene or vulgar notes is revolting and intolerable. Stop writing dirty notes — period!

"We are concerned about the large number of girls whose general behavior is becoming increasingly unfeminine and boy like. Girls who greet us by pushing us, hitting us, pounding us on the back, chasing us or mussing up our hair or clothing leave us absolutely cold. Try just saying hello.

"Girls who ask us if we love them, if we'll go steady with them, or if we'll date them are unappealing. If we want to be with you, we'll let you know. Don't call us, we'll call you.

"Girls who run everywhere all day and who come out in skirts at noon and try to play basketball or football with boys turn us off. Girls' athletics are great but pay attention to time, place and costume.

"Girls who smoke, ditch classes, shoplift, and hitch-hike are well known to all of us and respected by NONE of us. Suggestion: Don't smoke, attend school, pay for things you need and walk where you are going."

The proclamation concluded with an announcement that girls failing to comply with it would be subjected to a "total boycott of all friendly relations" with the 39 boys. The boycott started with the posting of the proclamation on the school bulletin board Friday morning with the hearty approval of the school principal and boys' counselor.

All girls got a copy in the home rooms and they all froze. They were still mad all-day Monday but by Tuesday they showed so much improvement, particularly in connection with underwear that the boycott was lifted pending a Girl-Watcher's meeting Friday.

Well, here is the young man's viewpoint, but men of all ages pretty much feel the same way.

1. Feminine Manner. The feminine manner is the motions of a woman's body, the way she uses her hands, her walk, her talk, the sound of her voice, her facial expressions, and her laugh. It is more important than that of appearance, for it is an even greater contrast to masculine strength and firmness.

David Copperfield was fascinated by Dora's enchanting manner; the way she patted the horses, spanked her little dog, or held her flowers against her chin were attractive to him. "She had the most delightful little voice, the gayest little laugh, the pleasantest and most fascinating little ways."

I have pointed out the importance of a feminine appearance in winning the notice of men, but if you do not add to this a feminine manner, the total effect can be disappointing but could end up even humorous.

For example, if you put a frilly feminine dress on a woman who has a stiff, brusque manner and a manly commanding voice, she just doesn't fit the dress. We have all seen women who wear the most feminine outfit but who wear them as if they were on the wrong person. They do not carry themselves generally in a way to harmonize with their clothes. They are professors in chiffon, bears in lace, or wooden posts in organdie. You will, therefore, have to add to a feminine appearance a beautiful enchanting manner, if you are to be attractive to men.

A Glimpse into Femininity

In the novel The Cloister and the Hearth by Charles Reade, is an illustration of the thrilling sensation the feminine manner can awaken in a man.

"Then came a little difficulty: Gerard could not tie his ribbon again as Catherine (his mother) had tied it. Margaret, after slyly eyeing his efforts for some time, offered to help him; for at her age girls love to be coy and tender, saucy and gentle by turns . . . then a fair head, with its stately crown of auburn curls, glossy and glowing through silver, bowed sweetly towards him; and while it ravished his eye, two white supple hands played delicately upon the stubborn ribbon and molded it with soft and airy touches. Then a heavenly thrill ran through the innocent young man and vague glimpses of a new world of feeling and sentiment opened to him.

And these new exquisite sensations Margaret unwittingly prolonged; it is not natural to her sex to hurry ought that pertains to the sacred toilet. Nay, when the taper fingers had at last subjugated the ends of the knot, her mind was not quite easy till, by a maneuver peculiar to the female hand, she had made her palm convex and so applied it with a gentle pressure to the center of the knot — a sweet little coaxing hand kiss, as much as to say, 'now be a good knot and stay so!' 'There, that was how it was!' said Margaret, and drew back to take one last survey of her work; then looking up for simple approval of her skill, received full in her eyes a longing gaze of such adoration as made her lower them quickly and color all over."

This experience between Gerard and Margaret conveys the tremendous feeling that a woman can awaken in a man, and in this case, it was accomplished by the feminine manner alone, principally the hands. You can imagine how fascinating a girl becomes when she adds to this a gentle voice, sweet expressions and soft looks. The feminine manner is one of the most important tools a woman can use in being attractive to men.

How to Acquire Feminine Manner

You acquire a feminine manner by accentuating the differences between yourself and men, not the similarities. Since men are strong, tough, firm and heavy in manner, women should be delicate, tender, gentle and light. We show this by our walk, voice, hands and the way we carry ourselves generally.

1. The Hands. Dora and Margaret charmed men with the use of their hands. Gentle motions, pats and maneuvers are peculiar to the female hand. Learn how to shake hands with men. Do so with gentleness and just enough firmness to convey friendship. Never shake a man's hand with strength and vigor, regardless of how happy you may be to see him. Take a man's arm lightly and never use him as a support. To do so makes you appear as a block of wood. Avoid stiff, brusque movements, waving the hands in the air or using them firmly in expressing yourself.

Never pound on the table to put over a point, and never grip the sides of a lecturer's stand. Also avoid slapping anyone on the back.

2. The Walk. Your manner of walking should be light. Imagine that you are light as a feather. Walk with knees slightly straight. This also encourages lightness and will make your walk cute and feminine. Keep head back over the spine, chest and chin high. Avoid slanting forward, rounding the shoulders or walking with knees bent, since this makes you appear heavy and matronly. Also avoid a heavy gait or long steps like men take.

3. The Voice. With your appearance and your manner contributing to your femininity, you must be careful that the good effect is not spoiled by your voice. Usually a girl who is practicing her walk and use her hands correctly will automatically modulate her voice to harmonize with her manner. If you discover that your voice might spoil the impression you are endeavoring to create, take a little time and effort to change it.

The ideal feminine voice is gentle and variable, with a clear ringing tone and an air of self-assurance. It is not a voice which is overly soft and timid, for these qualities suggest a lack of self-assurance, something unattractive in women. The main thing to avoid is loudness, firmness or any of the qualities like men have. Do not let your voice suggest mannish efficiency, coarse boldness or the ability to "kill your own snakes."

The voice should be just as appealing to the man's chivalrous desire to protect and shelter as the girl herself. No man likes a course, loud or vulgar tone in a woman any more than a woman likes an effeminate tone in a man. And no man likes a mumbling, dull, monotonous or singsong voice.

To speak correctly, speak with teeth apart. Pronounce consonants clearly and be expressive. A beautiful voice also has a ringing quality rather than a flat, dull sound.

4. The Laugh. It is more difficult for a person to change his laugh, although the tone will improve with the improvement of the ringing qualities of the voice. Avoid men's laughs, such as loudness or a deep tone.

Also avoid facial contortions, opening the mouth wide, throwing the head back, and slapping your hands on your thighs, roaring or anything coarse or vulgar. If these extremes are avoided the laugh will be acceptable.

5. The Cooing or Purring Quality. This is an extremely feminine quality. Deruchette "made all kinds of gentle noises, murmurings of unspeakable delight to certain ears." It is an intimate type of conversation that is soothing and feminine.

6. Facial Expressions. You have no better means of conveying femininity than through tender smiles, gentle eyes and sweet expressions. The opposite — harshness, bitterness, fierce frowns and tightness across the lip — all destroy feminine charm. Girls who are usually dainty and feminine, who suddenly take on a hard expression, always disappoint, like an unhappy ending to a beautiful story.

Femininity has its real roots in character, in a virtue called "a gentle tender quality." If you have a gentle character, it will naturally be conveyed through sweet expressions. If you do not, if you tend to be harsh and critical, to lose patience with people, it will be difficult to keep these traits hidden from view, to keep them from spoiling your femininity.

Be gentle and tender with everyone — your roommates, family and close friends — not just the men in your life. If you are one thing to a man and another to your friends, there will be times you will betray your double standard.

One last thought: When men offend you, I am not implying that you be bland or unresponsive, only that you not be bitter or harsh. A later chapter will explain how you can react to a man's irritating offenses with a charm called childlike sauciness.

7. Conversation. You can do a great deal to strengthen your feminine image through conversation. If someone unfortunate is the topic for discussion, you can show sympathy and love. Do not make the mistake of giving an unsympathetic remark like "Well, he deserves it," or "He had it coming to him." Take every opportunity to defend people, to be long suffering and understanding, and in this way show your gentle feminine nature.

Avoid talking about people you dislike lest you be tempted to make some unkind remark. Also avoid subjects which may lead to heated arguments. By avoiding negative statements and concentrating on positive expressions, you can do a great deal to enhance your femininity and therefore your attractiveness.

Refinement

One of the marks of a feminine woman is refinement. This means that she has "good social breeding" and sensitivity to the feelings of others, that she never deliberately offends anyone by being rude, impolite, inconsiderate, crude or socially negligent. She is tactful, diplomatic and considerate.

To be refined, you must never use coarse or vulgar language, profane, swear, tell vulgar jokes, etc. What these habits do to your character is one thing but what they do to your feminine image is more serious.

Although these coarse habits are not becoming in men either, they are somehow worse in women. Here again, men expect women to be even more refined creatures than men. Indulging in loud, coarse or vulgar talk not only causes a woman to fall from her pedestal but to fall from being the ideal of femininity in men's eyes. Men have always expected it should beneath feminine dignity to utter coarse language. They are naturally disappointed, if not repulsed, by a display of crudeness.

Still another mark of refinement is to show a courteous appreciation for everyone you meet, regardless of age, situation, financial or social standing. Every person entitled to respect. The higher your conception of human beings generally, the higher will be your tendency to be refined. To show a lack of courteous appreciation of anyone is only to show a decline in the quick intelligence and perception expected of a cultured person. Nothing is more quickly calculated to give you a coarse, unrefined character than to ignore or shun another individual.

In order to demonstrate a real consideration for people, it will be essential that you never do anything deliberately to hurt their feelings. Never, for example, show indifference for the opinions of another, or downgrade things he says or does, especially things he considers important. Be considerate of all the feelings, opinions, accomplishments, ideas, traditions, religious customs, or "ways of life" of others.

If, for example, you happen to meet a little old lady who has spent a lifetime devoted to a worship of traditions, don't show disrespect for her feelings by trampling on those traditions. Or if you have dinner with some honest soul who takes pride in her cooking, don't refuse it or give any indication that you are any less than delighted with her meal.

If you are in the home of an exceptionally cultured or refined person, do not show a disregard for her way of life by boisterous conduct or heated arguments. On the other hand, if the hostess is fun loving and set on everyone relaxing and having a good time, show consideration for her thinking by being light-hearted yourself. The greatest mark of refinement you can show is a genuine delight in the company you keep with a respect and consideration for their way of living.

Learn to respect another person's enthusiasm. For example, if a gentleman happens to be telling you of an adventurous journey he is about to take and gets into a state of excitement as he unfolds the plans, do not disappoint his enthusiasm by acting coldly indifferent or bored. Even worse, do not make a negative remark which would destroy his fervor altogether, such as reminding him how expensive or foolhardy it might be.

Or if he is merely eating a piece of pie which he enjoys heartily, do not make a cold remark like "How could you stand that kind?" Still another lack of refinement is "cheekiness," an old-fashioned word which means to be nervy or to impose on people.

Cheekiness is an attitude of "expecting" favors, with a lack of consideration for the imposition it might be on the other person. Some people are guilty of this practice by asking for things to eat while in the homes of their friends, or by asking to borrow clothing, perfume, cars or even money. This is not to say that there are not emergencies when we are justified in asking these favors, or that others are not willing to grant them, but borrowing is ordinarily considered rude and unrefined.

Be tactful and diplomatic in your remarks to people. Blunt honesty is never appropriate. Anything which must be said can be said with a kindly consideration for the other person. Refined women never ignore social invitations without a thoughtful acceptance or apology. They are courteous, with a respect for the feelings of everyone.

Timid Fearlessness

This is little understood by women today, and yet it is a most bewitching charm of womanhood. It can be described as an air of timid fearlessness, of self-conscious modesty and of pretty confusion. In order to understand this feminine trait, let us refer again to the incident of Rebecca Sharp, when she had just rebuked Joseph for tricking her into eating hot peppers.

When Joseph apologized with "No, I wouldn't hurt you for the world," she said, "No, I know you wouldn't," "and then she gave him ever so gentle a pressure with her little hand, and drew it back quite frightened, and looked first for one instant in his face and then down at the carpet rods, and I am not prepared to say that Joe's heart did not thump at this involuntary, timid, gentle motion of regard on the part of the simple girl." "And Oh," exclaims Thackeray, "what a mercy it is that women do not exercise their powers oftener! We can't resist them if they do."

Men are never quite prepared for such an unexpected, mysterious feminine maneuver, which is so very different from their own nature. This is perhaps why they are so fascinated by it.

Another illustration of timid fearlessness is found in the incident I referred to in The Cloister and the Hearth. In reviewing this incident, notice the trustfulness with which Margaret undertakes the intimate task of tying the strange young man's tie, the confiding, innocent attention to her work until the task is completed, then the sudden self-consciousness and appearance of timidity, modesty and pretty confusion when Gerard gazes at her in adoration.

You can practice timid fearlessness around men by first unconsciously performing some task, then when you realize that the man is noticing you, suddenly becoming self-conscious and confused. Look first directly up in his face for a moment, and then hastily down or to the side. Devise different ways to practice this dainty little skill under many circumstances. There is nothing like it to contrast your girlish modesty with the man's insensibility, not only to make the man conscious of your femininity, but even more pleasant to him, conscious of his own contrasting manhood, before which young girls tend to become self-conscious.

Bewitching Languor

Languor is a feminine characteristic and is a relaxed, calm, quiet air, similar to that of a cat relaxing before a fireplace. It is like a touch of velvet and is calming and appealing to men.

"Deruchette had at times an air of bewitching languor." Languor is a means of varying other feminine mannerisms. The opposite of languor is the nervous, high-strung woman who is always biting fingernails, jingling her keys, twisting her handkerchief or twisting her hair.

Now, as we come to the end of this section on the feminine manner, here are some do's and don'ts to follow:

Do's and Don'ts for Feminine Manner

Don't

1. Don't use your hands in a stiff, brusque, efficient, firm or strong manner.

2. Don't walk with a heavy gait, long steps, round shoulders or slanting forward.

3. Avoid the following qualities in the voice: loudness, firmness, efficiency, boldness, over-softness or timidity, dullness, flat tone, mumbling, monotonous singsong.

4. Don't laugh loudly or in a vulgar manner.

5. Don't use facial expressions that are hard, harsh, or bitter.

6. Don't indulge in words or conversation that are harsh, bitter, critical, impatient, crude, vulgar or unrefined.

7. Don't slap people on the back.

8.Don't whistle loudly.

9. Don't yell except in an emergency.

10. Don't talk loudly.

11. Don't roar at jokes.

12. Don't gulp food or eat noisily.

13. don't drink by throwing your head back.

14. Don't sit with legs apart or with one leg horizontal across the other.

Do

1. Use hands lightly

2. Take a man's arm lightly

3. Shake hands with men lightly

4. Walk evenly with knees slightly bent

5. Acquire a ringing tone to the voice, also gentleness, tenderness and self-assurance.

6. Acquire facial expressions that are gentle and tender.

7. In both words and conversation, speak with tenderness, gentleness and show kindness, patience, sympathy and love.

8. Eat quietly

9. Sit modestly

10. Be refined.

11. React with timid fearlessness.

Chapter 13

Feminine Dependency

Feminine dependency is a definite quality found in a truly feminine woman, a sort dependency upon men for their masculine care and protection. More than anything else it is a lack of masculine ability, a lack of aggressiveness, competency, efficiency, strength and the desire to "kill your own snakes."

You will remember in our studies of understanding men that we recognize men as guides, protectors and providers.

This they were designed to be. We were designed to be women, to be wives and mothers and therefore in need of masculine help. This need of masculine help and protection is called feminine dependency. This is not to be confused with general weakness. The quality is very attractive to men.

Dora was rather dependent upon men and for this reason made a strong appeal to David's gentlemanly heart. Agnes was too lacking in this quality. She was too self-sufficient, independent and too able to kill her own snakes to win David first.

Do not think that protecting a dependent woman is an imposition on a man. The most pleasant sensation a real man can experience is his consciousness of the power to give his manly care and protection. Rob him of this sensation of superior physical strength and ability and you rob him of his manliness.

It is a delight to him to protect and shelter a dependent woman. The bigger, manlier and more sensible a man is, the more he seems to be attracted to this quality.

How Men Feel in the Presence of Capable Women

What happens when the average red-blooded man comes in contact with an obviously manly, intellectual and competent woman manifestly independent of any help a "mere" man can give? He simply doesn't feel masculine around her any longer. In the presence of supposed manly strength and ability in a woman, he feels like an ineffectual imitation of a man. It is the most uncomfortable and humiliating sensation a man can experience; so that the woman who arouses it often becomes repugnant to him.

A man cannot derive any joy or satisfaction from protecting a woman who behaves as though she can obviously do very well without him. He only delights in protecting or sheltering a woman who needs or at least desires his manly care.

How Men Feel in the Presence of Dependent Women

When a man is in the presence of a tender, gentle, trustful woman, he immediately feels a sublime expansion of his power to protect and shelter this gentle and feminine creature.

In the presence of such womanliness he feels stronger, more competent, bigger, and manlier than ever. This feeling of strength and power is one of the most enjoyable he can experience. The apparent need of a woman for protection, instead of arousing contempt for her lack of ability, appeals to the very noblest feelings within him.

Amelia

A perfect illustration of feminine need in woman is in the character of Amelia in Vanity Fair. The following is a description of her and the charm she possessed in men's eyes.

"Those who formed the small circle of Amelia's acquaintances were quite angry with the enthusiasm with which the other sex regarded her. For almost all men who came near her loved her; though no doubt they would be at a loss to tell you why. She was not brilliant, nor witty, nor wise overmuch, nor extraordinarily handsome. But wherever she went she touched and charmed everyone of the male sex, as invariably as she awakened the scorn and incredulity of her own sisterhood. I think it was her weakness which was her principle charm; a kind of sweet submission and softness which seemed to appeal to each man she met for his sympathy and protection."

Mrs. Woodrow Wilson

Mrs. Wilson was a tender woman, for her husband wrote to her: "What a source of steadying and of strength it is to me in such seasons of too intimate self-questioning to have one fixed point of confidence and certainty — that even, unbroken, excellent perfection of my little wife, with her poise, her easy capacity in action, her unfailing courage, her quick efficient thought — and the charm that goes with it all, the sweetness, the feminine grace, — none of the usual penalties of efficiency — no hardness, no incisive sharpness, no air of command or of unyielding opinion. Most women who are efficient are such terrors."

The Efficient Woman that Men Admire

Occasionally, we may notice men who seem to admire women who are extremely efficient and capable in a manly way. Don't let this confuse you. Although many men may have a genuine admiration for such a woman, it does not mean he finds her attractive. He undoubtedly admires her as he would another man — with appreciation of her fine ability.

The All Too Capable Woman

There are many women, in all walks of life, who possess great personal magnetism, whom all, including the men, admire as great and powerful characters, but who can never change a man's admiration into romantic love. One such woman, a famous Sunday school teacher of young men and women, illustrates this situation. Her magnetic personality and noble character were so much admired that hundreds of young people sought to join her class and thousands of men and women of all ages attended whenever she gave a public lecture.

In spite of this almost universal respect and admiration, the average man would never think of seeking her private company, indulging in an intimate conversation or of making her his "little girl" to cherish and protect throughout a lifetime. Everyone knows of such women, healthy, charming, enjoyable, whom men admire greatly but whom they do not seem to be fascinated by. The reason for this is that they lack an air of feminine need for a masculine man. They are too capable and independent to stir a man's sentiments. This air of being able to kill your own snakes is what destroys the charm of so many business and professional women, and it is the absence of this air that permits many unsophisticated, artless women to win the heart an intelligent and capable man.

The kind of woman a man wants is first an angelic being whom a man can adore and think of as infinitely better than himself, but also an adorably little creature whom he would want to gather up in his arms and cherish and protect forever. The efficient women that we just mentioned fulfill the first requirement but fail to fulfill the second.

Though it is absolutely necessary to fulfill the first, you cannot afford to do as these women do and neglect the second.

If You Are A Big, Strong and All Too Capable Woman

What if you happen to be a big, strong and capable woman, or have a powerful personality or in some other way overpower men? How, then, can you possibly appear to be tender, trustful, delicate and dainty?

In the first place, size has nothing to do with the quality of femininity. No matter what your size, your height or your capabilities, you can appear girly to a man if you follow certain rules and if you will take on an attitude of womanliness. It is not important that you actually be little and delicate, but that you seem so to the man you love.

When the Large Woman Attracts the Smaller Man

Occasionally we will see a rather small short man happily married to a large woman. It is interesting to observe that she does not seem large to him because she has given him the impression of smallness. Such a man might call her "his little girl." She has managed, in spite of her size, to give him the impression of delicacy. By letting him know that she can't get along without him, that she is dependent upon him to protect her from danger, he has been able to disguise her large and seemingly overpowering figure.

If you are a large, tall or strong woman you might want to work to disguise these features so that the man you love will have the impression that you are delicate. As you begin to develop your feminine nature, the one you were born with, you will tend to lose some of your more masculine qualities and supplant them with true femininity.

Little Fears

Another trait of femininity is being subject to little fears and uneasiness in the presence of real or imagined dangers. Feminine women, for example, are known to be afraid of bugs, mice, the dark, strange noises, etc., much to the amusement of men. In the presence of her trepidation he naturally feels stronger. If she shrinks from a spider or hops on a chair at the sight of a mouse, how manly he feels that he can laugh at such trembling and calm her fears. It does a man almost as much good to save a woman from a mouse than a tiger, since he feels so masculine.

Feminine women are also known to be afraid of the dangers of nature. An illustration of this is in the following incident a woman confided to me.

Her husband owned a sailboat and was a competent seaman. He loved to take her into dangerous waters and heel the boat over on its side. She was terrified at such times and asked me, "Why does he do this when he knows I am afraid?" I explained that the very reason he does is because she is so afraid, and he is so unafraid. Her fearfulness was attractive to him. I encouraged her to not try to control her fearfulness, to reveal it in more calm waters, and perhaps he would be satisfied and not take her out further. It would be a mistake for a woman to subdue the tendency of her little fears in the presence of masculine men. To do so would be to rob herself of one of her elements of real charm.

You Need Not Be Beautiful to Be Feminine

You need not be beautiful to have all of the charms of femininity. There are thousands of rather average girls who succeed in being attractive to men because they are models of femininity. On the other hand, there are thousands of other women who are traditionally beautiful in their faces and features but who, because of masculinity of their manner, never impress men as being especially attractive. When a girl is tender, soft, fun-loving, lovable and also innocent and pure, who stops to inquire if she has beauty in the classical sense?

Regardless of her feature or form, to most men she will seem a paragon of delicious femininity. To them she is beautiful!

Even when a woman is homely, men can be attracted nevertheless. While they may not consider her traditionally beautiful, they may consider her pert, cute, charming, dainty, lovable and saucy and everything else that is highly fascinating. Sometimes such a woman has the most enchanting personality of all and succeeds in captivating the most desirable men. Such a woman can make a merely beautiful woman seem insignificant beside her. You must not let the absence of beauty discourage you; nor must you let the possession of beauty, if you have it, lull you into a false security. The presence or the absence of beauty is of minor consequence in the attainment of true femininity.

How to Develop Feminine Need for Masculinity

In acquiring this feminine need, stop doing things that are very masculine. Stop lifting very heavy objects, moving furniture, mowing the lawn, fixing motors, changing tires, balancing on tall ladders, or anything else along this line that you may be doing.

Stop doing these things whether you are in the presence of men or not unless it is an emergency. Let men take care of the things that belong in their world where possible. Then also stop being too aggressive, dominating men or bossing them around.

Also, if you are in love with a man, don't be competitive with him or deliberately try to excel him in his own field.

For example, don't try to outdo him in sports, in lifting weights, in running, in repairing equipment, etc.

The next rule is: Need his manly care and protection. Remember, a man does not enjoy protecting a woman who obviously doesn't need him. He delights in protecting or helping a woman who needs or wants his manly care.

So, in every way you can, indicate to him that you do need his masculine assistance. First, "always accept his chivalry when offered." Let him open doors for you, help you with your coat, pull up your chair, lift your boxes or books, help you over a creek bed, offer you his coat in the cold or a rainstorm, give you his seat on the bus, run errands for you, help you solve a problem or wait upon you for this or that.

As often as you can, accept a man's offer to help you. Be sure to thank him and let him know how much it was appreciated and needed. If a man does not offer his help in a rainstorm or at a creek bed you might try this: either shiver in the cold or hesitate fearfully at the creek bed. Or ask him for his assistance.

Ask him to open jar lids for you, or to lift a heavy object, or to advise you on a difficult problem or to help you with an assignment. Remember that it is not an imposition on a man to ask him for his masculine assistance. Men enjoy helping women because it makes them feel masculine.

In every way you can, demonstrate your need for him and let him know either by asking or by some outward appearance of your feminine need of his assistance.

The next rule is this: If at some time or another you are stuck with a masculine job in the presence of men, do it in a feminine manner.

For example, if you must lift a heavy sack of groceries, or must change a tire, or hammer some nails, do so with all womanliness. This means to struggle with it or show some lack of skill. It is not up to you to perform masculine tasks with the same skill that men do. They will never come to your rescue if you can do these things as well as they can. Be yourself, your true feminine self, and he will come quickly to the rescue because you appear in need of his help.

Developing Feminine Need

1. Dispense with a masculine air of strength and ability and acquire a feminine attitude.

2. Stop doing masculine things where possible.

3. Don't be competitive with the man you love in his masculine field or try to excel him.

4. Don't be ashamed to need men and call on them when needed.

5. If stuck with a masculine job, do it in a feminine manner.

Practice your femininity on every man you meet until it becomes second nature to you. The kind of women who are most universally attractive look upon men as big and strong. Truly feminine women do actually feel the contrast between themselves and every man for his strength and masculine capabilities.

What Feminine Need for A Man Awakens in Him

The air of delicacy and need awakens in a man — tenderness. As he begins to do things for you, to shelter you, wait upon you, take care of you, the tenderness grows. Your very need of care has contributed to this feeling of tenderness.

A woman needs also to care for the man she loves, to help him, to comfort him, to watch over him and keep others from taking unfair advantage of him. Thus, she too feels that he is dependent upon her in a different sort of way, and she too delights in his need of her and of her ability to fill the need of such a big, strong man. She too feels tenderness towards the one she is caring for.

Summary

As we come to the end of the chapter on femininity, you should have gained a new insight into the subject. Femininity, as you can see, is much more than just ruffles and lace. Although a feminine appearance is important, it is of little use without the feminine manner; and neither of them will be of any merit without the beautiful quality of feminine need for the man you love.

Of all the qualities a woman may possess, this one attribute outweighs them all. It will make a woman enchanting, cuddlesome, lovable and fascinating in men's eyes and altogether too bewitching to be allowed to go through life without the care and protection of a man.

Without femininity you may have a magnetic personality and you may have a powerful character, but in men's eyes you will not be a feminine woman. Men aren't interested in a great and powerful character. He wants a woman.

Remember: The main way you achieve femininity is by accentuating the differences between you and men and by needing their manly care and assistance.

Radiant Happiness

I have already told you of inner happiness which is a spiritual quality. What then is radiant happiness? Radiant happiness is a human quality and is part of charm. It is such things as cheerfulness, laughter, singing, joyfulness, smiles, bright eyes, pleasant outlooks, hope, optimism and the ability to radiate happiness to others.

Radiant happiness is one of the real charms that men find fascinating in women, counting far more than physical beauty of face and form. Beautiful girls should not make the mistake of hoping their pretty faces alone will win the attention of men. Without a smile and sparkling eyes your allurement will be limited. Men admire pretty girls, but they more often search for radiant smiling women to be their companions.

Women who lack beauty of face and form due to irregular features, sometimes turn out to be real charmers because they have worked diligently to acquire the qualities that really count with men. Amelia, you will remember, was chubby and stout, with a short nose and round cheeks, yet she succeeded in winning the love of many men who came near her. This was due to her smiling lips, eyes and heart.

There is great emphasis in our modern times upon appearance, especially of clothes, hair styles, etc. This emphasis upon the "outer shell" is all very good, but if radiance is not also added it will be like serving a beautiful banquet, arranging the table with the finest china, silver and crystal, and then serving bland food. For example, a girl can be dressed in the latest styles from the most expensive salons, with her hair arranged in the most feminine and alluring fashion, but if she also appears with a disagreeable or sour expression on her face she will be a "flop" as far as men are concerned.

If, on the other hand, she appears in rather plain clothing and hair style, but a smile of radiance included, let a good man catch her eye and he will be fascinated, and her ordinary appearance will not mean as much in comparison with the beauty of her face.

This is not to underestimate the value of feminine and girlish clothes, etc., but only to stress that unless radiance is added, the effect will fail to be as fascinating as it could be.

Deruchette, Amelia And Dora

The most fascinating trait of Deruchette was her ability to radiate happiness to others, to "shed joy around" and "cast light upon dark days." She had in her smile alone a "power" which was great enough to lift the spirits of others. She radiated joy to her entire household, for her presence alone brought "light" to the household and her approach was like cheerful warmth. As the author says, "she passes by and we are content; she stays awhile and we are happy."

Amelia was "kind, fresh and smiling, with a smiling heart." Dora had a "gay little laugh and a delightful little voice." Mrs. Woodrow Wilson also had this quality, for her husband said, "She was so radiant, so happy!"

Men simply aren't as comfortable with women who are glum, depressed, or even overly serious.
They are more attracted to women who are vibrant, alive and happy!

Dolly Madison

The longest reigning and one of the most cheerful of all first ladies of the White House was Dolly Madison. During the eight years her husband presided she won the hearts of her countrymen and was known as the most popular person in the United States. In a Parisian turban topped with a plume, her neck and arms strung with pearls, she was the perfect hostess — bubbly and natural, tactful and gracious. Her zest for life seemed to never run out.

One day at age 82 she simply passed from a nap to death. "She sparkled," reported a friend, "up to the very verge of the grave."

Ninon De Lenclos

Ninon de Lenclos of the 17th century courts of France was another woman of special charm and radiance. Some of the greatest men of the century loved her, and she is said to have won the hearts of three generations of men in a single family, for she lived and retained her beauty and charm into her eighties.

Some of the most interesting women of France were her devoted friends. The most wonderful thing about her, everyone said, was her eager delight in everything around her. In her own words she said, "You never hear me say 'this is good or this is bad,' but a thousand times a day I say 'I enjoy, I enjoy.'"

How to Acquire Radiant Happiness

While you are working on happiness becoming a habit, apply radiance wherever you can. It is surprising what you can do by conscious effort. A good suggestion is the following: After you have applied your makeup, stand before the mirror for a few seconds and practice radiance. Remember, your artful makeup will not be as effective if you wear a glum expression. If you leave the room with a happy face your friends or family will be apt to reflect back this same expression, and your day will begin with good spirit and charm.

The radiance, however, must be of the lips, the eyes and the entire countenance and not just a stiff wooden-like smile. After this good beginning, add a cheerful, optimistic attitude. Try not to be skeptical or dubious about life in general. Our attitude should be one of optimism, hope and emphasis on the brighter side of life. It will be difficult to have a smile such as Deruchette, which has the "power to lift the spirits of others," unless we also maintain a bright outlook. Radiate your happiness to all and not merely those who are already pleasant. Deruchette "shed joy around," which suggests that she shed it to everyone as the rain that falls on every flower in the forest, not just a select few.

Radiate not only to the happy, but also to the sad, the depressed and disconsolate. The world delights in sunny people; there are more than enough of the negative ones. A bright smile does more good for the downhearted than food for the hungry.

Then give sunshine to the frowning, sour and disagreeable also. They need it the most of all. Give whether you believe deserving or not. Your smile will be even more appreciated because it is such a rare pleasure with those who frown. A soft look can soften the hardest heart, so don't underestimate the value of your upbeat disposition to such people. They will credit it as a mark of a womanly woman.

If you practice radiance upon all you meet, the deserving and the no so deserving, you will acquire it as a habit and it will then seem natural to you.

If you do not show it to all, but only to those you are attracted to, your happiness may appear as "flirting" and you may be suspected of man hunting.

Demure

There is another word that is always in good men's hearts when speaking of attractive womanhood — the word demure. The meaning of the word in connection with attractive womanhood is an air of radiant happiness mixed with playful mischievousness. The perfect illustration is of a woman who is radiantly alive and playful but who puts on an act of gravity, the comers of her lips struggling to suppress a smile of mischief and her eyes dancing in an otherwise grave face. This playful contrivance is attractive to men.

Smiling Through Adversity

As with the nature of life, we all have times when we become discouraged. It is then that smiling seems much more difficult. Not only is it difficult but may seem unnatural. However, there is always something to be grateful for and feel positive about. It is a mark of true character, especially womanly character, to smile in the face of adversity. The following lines by Ella Wheeler Wilcox express this trait beautifully:

It is easy enough to be pleasant When life flows by like a song.

But the one worthwhile is the one who can smile When everything goes dead wrong. For the test of the heart is trouble and it always comes with the years. And the smile that is worth the praises of earth Is the smile that shines through tears.

When to Not Smile

There are some occasions when it is best not to express an overabundance of cheerfulness. For example, when you are in the presence of someone who is depressed, your happy attitude may suggest a lack of sympathy. In this case it would be best to show kindness and compassion and show an understanding for what the other person is suffering. Try to be perceptive of these situations in which gravity and sympathy seem more appropriate. You can tell by the reaction of the person. If they seem offended by your buoyancy, they will likely feel it is not in harmony with their low spirits.

The Real Charm

Inner happiness combined with radiant happiness is an essential part of the real charm that men find fascinating in women. As we have learned, it brings a calm spirit and tranquility which is a peaceful beauty. It is like clear calm water in a pond. Radiant happiness is like lily pads that add breathtaking beauty. Beneath the flowers you can see the stillness of the waters. The charm is in the overall effect.

Fresh Radiant Health

The foundation of fresh beauty is genuine good health, not only for the health itself, but for the fresh and joyous spirit it sustains in the woman's appearance, actions and attitude. How alluring are sparkling and dancing eyes, lustrous hair, clear voice, buoyancy of manner and the animation which good health brings to the face and the vivacity it communicates to the thoughts.

We all know the importance of good health, but our trouble lies in thinking of good health in terms of not being ill. The perfection of healthy womanhood is more than merely being well. A fresh radiant appearance is a result of health in rich abundance. Health, like happiness, is based upon laws. It comes as a result of understanding and applying them. The following are the fundamentals of good health:

1. Correct internal disorders where possible.

2. Get enough sleep.

3. Exercise.

4. Drink plenty of water.

5. Get fresh air.

6. Eat properly.

7. Relax — at work or play.

8. Have a healthy mental attitude.

9. Control weight.

1. Correct Internal Disorders. It is difficult to attain the kind of health you want if there are internal disorders. Often women will go for years with such things as infected teeth, infected internal organs, disorders of the blood or glands and other malfunctions of the body which causes them to have poor health. Many of these ailments can be eliminated by proper attention.

2. Get Enough Sleep. We all know the value of sufficient sleep, but young women often neglect this essential due to heavy schedules of social life, work or studies. If you are robbed of your sleep by too many things to do, ask yourself if your activities are more important than you or your health. Many things we do are a waste of time when it comes right down to facts, especially when they are measured against genuine good health. The average woman needs between 6-8 hours a night.

3. Exercise. Exercise is as important as the food we eat in both preserving life and youth and in producing health. You may feel that you have enough exercise in the ordinary activities like walking, bending and reaching. These motions of the body do not bring into play all of the muscles. As a result, many women suffer from poor posture, weak muscles, fat deposits and loss of health. If exercise seems like merely an added labor to your

already busy schedule, remember that exercise can actually increase stamina.

4. Drink Plenty of Water. The body is made up of 66 percent water — more than two-thirds by weight and several gallons in all. If you do not drink enough water your body will be forced to use its water over and over again. Your whole system will suffer unless refreshed frequently with a new supply of water. If you drink eight 8-ounce glasses, which equals about 2 liters or a half gallon, this should be sufficient.

5. Get Fresh Air. A good air supply consists of three things. The first is having fresh air with ample oxygen content, the second is to breathe deeply enough to take the air into your lungs, and the third is to make certain that the air is not lacking in moisture.

Oxygen is important. What good food is to the stomach, oxygen is to the blood. You must therefore make sure that you have fresh air in your rooms and also that you breathe deeply enough to take it into your lungs. Poor posture and lack of exercise are responsible for shallow breathing, which leads to a shortage of oxygen in the blood. The purpose of exercise is not only the development of the muscles but also a healthy intake of air, deep into the lungs.

6. Eat Properly. What is a safe guide for proper eating? Our appetite is not a safe guide, for even bad foods can taste good.

There are many foods and products on the market. Which are good and which ones harmful? Many of the studies concerning foods are confusing and some of them are contradictory.

Nature reveals to us many of the secrets of good eating. We cannot improve on an apple as it comes from a tree, or a banana, or a potato as it comes from the earth. Eat foods as near to nature as possible is the safest rule.

There is fresh food available in every season. The summer brings its fruit, vegetables and melons; the fall brings apples, squash and potatoes which last until spring. Early spring brings navel oranges, late spring, berries and more fresh vegetables. All of these are best when eaten fresh in the season in which they grow. Nature also produces grains which remain fresh for several seasons.

Wholesome foods fall into five categories:

1. Fresh fruits
2. Fresh vegetables
3. Nuts
4. Grains
5. Meats

There are many highly processed and refined foods on the market today, many of them containing preservatives. They come in boxes, cans and packages. Some of the vital elements have been removed, and in an effort to make up for this lack, man has added his own created vitamins and minerals. Can man improve upon nature?

7. Relax. The secret of being able to relax at work or play is essential to both health and charm and is an ability which is fairly easy to acquire. The mind controls the body, and this control can cause either tension or relaxation. If you will learn

and practice meditation, you will immediately feel a relief of tension. This same technique can be applied in getting to sleep.

8. Have a Healthy Mental Attitude. The effect of prolonged attitudes such as worry, fear, anxiety, pessimism, hate, resentments, impatience, envy, anger, or any other irritating mental image can have a detrimental effect upon the human body. Its destructive influence is carried through the nervous system to the entire body. Even after the temporary emotion has left, the physical damage might remain.

A healthy mental attitude comes as a result of positive thinking.

In contrast, pro-active attitudes, buoyant and kindly thoughts, have exactly the opposite effect. Faith, optimism, love, kindness, cheerfulness, sympathy and enthusiasm all harmonize with body function and tend to invigorate the system.

9. Control Weight. Controlling weight is important not only for health but for self-esteem. You might want to consider a lifestyle change that includes healthier eating as well as exercise and all the above suggestions. Dieting suggests something temporary while changing the way you look at not only food, but exercise can help you with a permanent change in your life. Some women suffer from serious weight problems due to abuse or low self-esteem.

As you practice the principles of Fascinating Womanhood, you will find you have more confidence in tackling any problem such as your weight. You will better recognize your worth and your ability to be feminine, which will help you not only with men but with all your relationships. Good self-esteem is important in the art of being attractive and charming. There are many men who like women of various sizes. You can look fabulous at almost any size, but you still need to consider your health, not just your looks.

If Health Is Beyond Your Reach

There are some who, because of permanent damage, cannot attain this ideal of abundant health. If, however, they maintain a healthy mental attitude, they may appear much healthier than they actually are.

Elizabeth Barrett Browning was an invalid, yet one of the truly charming women in history. Her husband, Robert Browning, adored her. Her physical weakness was not an added attraction, but she had an abundance of other womanly qualities which overcame the physical lack.

Radiant health is only one qualification of Angela Human. If you have a healthy mental attitude you may still be a fascinating woman.

Cleanliness and Grooming

Good health is not the only essential in attaining a fresh appearance. Cleanliness and grooming are also important. The teeth, the hair, the nails, the feet, and cleanliness of the entire body are vital contributions to the effect of freshness. It would seem inconsistent with our ideal of Angela Human to expect her to be anything less than immaculate and well groomed.

Clothes

A fresh appearance in clothing is especially attractive such as fresh starched collars, flowers (real or artificial), polished shoes and clean, well pressed clothes contribute to a fresh look. Certain materials and colors appear fresh, while others are drab. Clean stripes, ginghams, and feminine prints suggest freshness.

Make-up

Most men are not opposed to artificial allurements if it makes the ear more alive and healthy. In fact, your attention ails only indicates to him your efforts to please him. Eye makeup and lipstick especially help to make the face appear bright and fresh, which is the reason they were created.

Chapter 16

Childlikeness

Little children have some qualities which we would do well to copy, and this we do with childlikeness. We copy the adorable traits of little girls, their tenderness, innocence, playfulness, spunk, sauciness, trustfulness and joyfulness.

Men love this trait in women. It amuses them, enchants and fascinates them because, like the other aspects of femininity, it is such a contrast to their own superior strength and masculine abilities.

We find this trait in our study of Dora, Amelia, and Deruchette. Dora was "captivating, bright eyed and girlish." Amelia had the tender emotions of a little child, for her eyes would quickly fill with tears. Deruchette had a "childlike prattle," and "she who was one day to become a mother was for a long while a child." She had the giddiness, vivacity and teasing playfulness of a little girl.

We will now devote ourselves to a study of this fascinating subject. The following are the different traits which make up childlikeness in women.

Sauciness

In our relationships with men they sometimes mistreat us. A man may, for example, be insulting, thoughtless, unkind, negligent or unfair; and if he is the mischievous type he may even tease us to the point of irritation. The usual response to this mistreatment is for the girl to become defensive or develop resentful attitude. These reactions are often unattractive to men and can cause problems in the relationship, at least temporarily. Sometimes a girl may make the mistake of becoming very angry. If she does, this could dampen her femininity. None of these reactions are attractive or successful in dealing with men.

A girl needs to be forgiving, of course, to overlook small errors and occasional thoughtlessness, but if she shows no reaction to thoughtless or continual mistreatment, this is an indication of a lack of self-dignity. The man, you can be sure, will not be impressed with her lack of sensitivity, for he will not appreciate a woman he can walk on, push around and mistreat. Most men admire women with spunk, who have enough pride and self-dignity to defend themselves against mistreatment.

When a girl is mistreated, it would be a mistake for her to set out to remake the man, to teach him that she expects to be treated better. It doesn't tend to work and only causes friction. All men need the freedom to be themselves and to act as their impulses dictate at the moment, whether their impulses happen to be right or wrong, wise or foolish.

Our responsibilities as women are to learn how to rect. The solution, however, is very simple. The way to react when a man is thoughtless is to show childlike sauciness. There is no better school for learning sauciness than watching the antics of little children, especially little girls. They are so trusting, so sincere, so innocent, and yet so outspoken that they are often teased into innocent anger. They are too childlike to feel hate, jealousy, resentment, and the uglier emotions. When such a child is teased she doesn't respond with biting sarcasm. Instead she might her foot, shake her curls or pout. Finally, she might threaten never to speak to you again, then peek back at you over her shoulder to see if you thought she really meant it, only to stamp her foot in impatience when she sees that you are not the least bit fooled.

One feels an irresistible longing to pick up such a child and hug her. We would do anything rather than to permit such an adorable little thing to suffer danger or want; to protect and care for such a delightfully human little creature would be nothing less than a delight.

This is much the same feeling that a woman inspires in a man when she is adorably angry. This extreme girlishness makes him feel in contrast, stronger, and so much more of a man. This is why women who are little spitfires, independent and saucy, are often sought after by men. This irritation, however, must be the sauciness of a child, and not the intractable stubbornness of a woman who would love to "get back" at anyone who might offend her.

How to Be Saucy

The key to childlike anger is this: Your spunk or sauciness must be mostly pretense. This fiery display of emotions must be only on the surface. They are absent of the deep emotions of hate, bitterness or resentment. Even from the beginning you understand his thoughtlessness is human and that no real injury was intended. If real pain is inflicted, another approach should be taken and childlikeness doesn't fit.

One thing to help you learn is to try ham acting. Pretend that you are in a play and must do a scene displaying childlike anger. Since you are not experienced or talented enough to portray these emotions, you must do so by exaggeration. This will come close to what we mean by pretense in childlike sauciness. Now, in learning this art, the following are some ideas which you can rely upon to help you.

1. Some Things to Do. One of the best ideas to start out with is to pout or protrude the lower lip. You can easily learn this art. Some other things you could try is to stomp your foot, shake your head, open your eyes wide, place both hands on your hips, or square your shoulders and lift your chin high. These are only a few of the signs of sauciness. You can discover many others on your own.

2. Exaggerate. Another thing to do is to exaggerate his treatment of you. Say, for example, "You are the most thoughtless man in town," or "So this is the way you treat a poor little helpless girl like me," or "Oh, what a dreadful thing to do!" Be sure to watch your words, that they represent a trustful feminine woman of good character and not a vulgar

suspicious one. Do not, for example, use words that are crude or insulting, such as nasty, wicked, dumb, ridiculous, hateful, rude, etc.

Also exaggerate your threats of punishment. For example, say, "I'll never speak to you again!" or "I won't do anything for you anymore," or "You're going to be sorry, you just wait and see!" or, "I'll tell my mother on you!"

3. Acquire a List of Adjectives. Have in your mind a list of adjectives which will be fitting for the occasion of sauciness and also which will complement the man's masculinity. Some suggestions are big, tough, brute, stubborn, obstinate, unyielding, inflexible, unmanageable, determined, unruly, hairy beast, stiff-necked, difficult, troublesome, and hardhearted. Be certain that your words compliment his masculinity and are not words that would crush his ego, such as little, wimp, pipsqueak, insignificant, weak, simple minded, etc.

It is interesting to note that the reason children tend to exaggerate in both their expressions and their bold words, is due to their feeling of helplessness in the presence of larger adults or even in the presence of other older children. Unconsciously, in a moment of frustration, they feel they must make up for their smallness by exaggerations. When a woman uses this method, she gives the man the impression that she is smaller, more vulnerable and therefore childlike. A good illustration of childlike sauciness is found in the story of David Copperfield. In this particular situation, Dora responded to David's criticism with the charms of both exaggerations and adjectives.

Dora's Anger

David had criticized Dora because she didn't manage the hired help well and because of this, one of them had stolen Dora's gold watch and fallen into further difficulty. He put the blame on Dora. The hired help was a young boy, called a page. "I began to be afraid," said David, "that the fault is not entirely on one side, but that these people all turn out ill because we don't turn out very well ourselves."

"Oh, what an accusation," exclaimed Dora, opening her eyes wide, "to say that you ever saw me take gold watches. Oh! Oh! you cruel fellow, to compare your affectionate wife to a transported page! Why didn't you tell me your opinion of me before we were married? Why didn't you say, you hard hearted thing, that you were convinced that I was worse than a transported, page? Oh, what a dreadful opinion to have of me! Oh, my goodness!"

Notice, she exaggerates and uses pet adjectives.

Becky Sharp

Another illustration of sauciness is found in the story of Vanity Fair, the story in which we find the character of Amelia. Becky Sharp also succeeded in charming men throughout the story. On the occasion I shall mention Amelia's brother, Joseph, had tricked Miss Becky into eating hot peppers. "I shall take good care how I let you choose for me another time," said Rebecca as they went down to dinner. "I didn't know men were fond of putting poor little harmless girls to pain" "By Gad,

Miss Rebecca, I wouldn't hurt you for the world" was Joseph's apology.

These three suggestions— childlike mannerisms, exaggerations, and masculine adjectives — will usually succeed in making the man amused, charmed, enchanted, and usually diffuse the situation bringing him to some kindly words of apology, as did Joseph to Rebecca, "I would not hurt you for the world." But if not, if the man persists in his amusement, is so enchanted that he teases you into further "anger."

4. Being Angry with Yourself. In order to explain this, let me refer again to the illustration of the little girl who became adorably angry with herself. Again, children, because of their relative smallness, feel they are no match for adults. In this little girl's moment of frustration, because she could not get the adult to apologize, she becomes irritated. The realization of her helplessness causes her to become angry with herself and saucier than ever.

Women who are saucy apply this same principle in their relationships with men. When their sauciness succeeds only in arousing the man's amusement, without an apology, they respond with self-anger, as much as to say, "What can a little girl like me do with a big overpowering man like you."

Young children who have this trait will sometimes stomp and fret and fume in the most amusing and adorable self-anger and even sometimes laugh at themselves for their inadequacy to get the best of men.

In applying this principle, one idea is to lift your chin high, and swish off. Then, when you reach the doorway, do as the little girl did, peek back over your shoulder. At this point the man will probably be smiling in amusement. If so, then stomp your foot in self-anger, lift your chin a little higher and swish off. There are many different variations of self-anger which you can learn by observation and also by practice. Here is an example of childlikeness and, though it occurred between married couples, the principles work exactly the same.

The Big Bully

We were in the mountains with another family. Even though it was not dinner time, both men said they were hungry and would like to have supper. They said they would go for a ride while we fixed it.

Dinner was ready on time, but our husbands did not return. In fact, they were two hours late. This gave me plenty of time to think about what I would say when they got back. I looked forward to their arrival to see if childlikeness would work for me.

When the men came in the door they were grinning sheepishly from the fun they had been having and yet realizing they were very late. I grabbed a pillow, threw it at my husband and said "You big bully! We stay behind slaving over a hot stove to fix a nice dinner for you and you don't even bother to come back and eat it! I'll never speak to you again!"

Both men grinned from ear to ear and I found a big smile on my own face, to my surprise. I had been very angry. We were having fun!

As soon as we finished eating my husband asked me to leave the dishes so he could show me the beautiful grove of trees in their autumn glory before dark. The other husband wanted to go with us so asked his wife to please watch all our children while we were gone. On our ride my husband was very attentive while his friend kept grinning and chuckling about my reaction when they came in late."

When to Be Saucy

When you have been irritated or provoked is the time to be saucy. If you feel within you the emotions of hate, bitterness or resentment, then it will be impossible for you to use childlike anger until you first calm down and get centered again. When you feel less intense emotions such as irritation, you will be able to respond like a little girl, and thereby express your offense and show your self-dignity and spunk.

Also, remember to react with sauciness only when you have been neglected or teased. Don't try to be saucy when it is someone else the man has offended. Only respond when you have been insulted, neglected or treated unfairly, or when he has been thoughtless of you. Also, you should not be saucy due to some negligence on his part that does not affect you, some mistake or error or failure that is in his world and that is really not your affair.

After you have studied the subject of sauciness until you feel that you understand it, practice it upon your family, your brothers and your father, or even your roommates. You will soon find that this charming art is a part of your feminine nature and therefore it will be natural to you. You may remember in the novel The Cloister and the Hearth the author said, "Girls like to be coy and tender, saucy and gentle by turns."

Our nature is to be not only feminine, but also saucy. You need only recapture that which belongs to you by nature and that which you had not so long ago when you were a little girl. And when you do evoke this charming art, you will find that men love it. They will be fascinated and captivated, to say nothing of being amused. This is due to the contrast between their manly and superior strength and capabilities and your girlishness.

Teasing Playfulness

Another charming art of childlikeness is "teasing playfulness." You can use this coquettish trait when a man is overly serious, stern or cross with you, or when he sits you down to give you a lecture on how you need to improve, etc. A perfect illustration of this is found in the character of Babbie in the play, The Little Minister.

The dignified little minister looked with unadulterated horror upon her wild gypsy ways. But when he protested with her about her apparent irresponsibility she interrupted the serious lecture by teasingly wanting to know which was the taller, making him stand back-to-back to measure their respective heights. And then, when he was ready to burst with indignation at her lack of seriousness, she pouted adorably as if to say "you're not really going to be angry with poor little me" and flashed at him such a confiding, trustful, I-am-certain-you-like-me-too-well-to-hurt-me glance and smile that the poor man forgot his indignation completely in a struggle with himself to keep from gathering the adorable creature in his arms and telling her, "No, I wouldn't want to hurt you for all the world."

Notice, the first thing that Babbie did was to change the subject by wanting to know who was taller. Then she distracted his attention away from his lecture by making him stand back-to-back with her. You can practice a similar teasing playfulness by following this same method.

First, change the subject to something playful and light, then distract his attention by such things as "adjusting his glasses," "straightening his tie," "smoothing his hair," etc. Make an effort to find ways and means to practice this charming art. Men will find it enchanting, and you will help to drive away the seriousness from life. And an unwanted and uncalled for lecture.

Teasing playfulness in women does not mean playing pranks. This trait is characteristic immaturity.

Tenderness of Emotion

Another trait men find especially attractive in women is tenderness of emotion like crying, sympathy and pity. Amelia, you may remember, "would cry over a dead canary," or "a mouse," or "the end of a novel." The tendency to cry is strong in young girls and usually carries over to adult life for many women. Don't make the mistake of smothering emotions too much while watching a dramatic or sad movie, or while listening to some inspiring music, or a moving story, or an incident which arouses your sympathy. Most men find these tender emotions attractive.

Girls who have this childlike trait of tenderness is easily excited to pity or sympathy. If a man, for example, is telling a story, or describing his experiences, the absorbedly interested girl gets into quite a state of excitement over what happens, sympathizes heartily with the characters involved, is horrified and delighted by turns, and can hardly wait for the end to find out if everyone escaped unhurt. This dainty betrayal of girlish tenderness of heart is highly entertaining and fascinating to men. They will sometimes concoct the wildest and most heart-rending tales just for the sake of stirring up her tender little heart. Not only is her eager sympathy attractive, but when she learns his story is all a product of his imagination, her childlike irritation, her air of saying "how could a big man like you deceive a little girl like me," her helpless fury at him for teasing her is even more amusing. Practice this bewitching art at every opportunity.

Another way a woman can show tenderness is when she is hurt or disappointed. As I have already explained in this chapter, sometimes a man is thoughtless, unfair, etc. The usual charming response is sauciness; but occasionally his remark will be entirely too cutting to react in any other way than crying. She might be just too hurt. If this is the case, it is helpful to adopt the adorable crying of little girls. She can, for example, quiver the lips, let a tear or two trickle down the cheeks, look with downcast eyes, twist her handkerchief, etc. This is good psychology, not manipulation as some might think. Why? Manipulation is about a person getting what they want without regard for another while good psychology is about the improvement of any relationship. It helps both equally.

Childlike Joy

We can also learn the art of childlike joy from watching little girls. Have you ever noticed a little girl when she has just been rewarded with a pleasant surprise or is promised some forthcoming good time? What does she do? She opens her eyes wide, claps her hands and might even jump up and down. The benefactor receives so much enjoyment in the presence of such eagerness that he is apt to repeat the act again and again, just to see the sparkle in her eyes and the joyfulness of her manner. It takes very little to make children happy which is why we appreciate their joy and want so much to do things for them. While you might not jump up and down, you can adopt some of the adorable responses from innocent children in expressing joy.

Exuberant women, who get all excited over every little thing, sometimes have men who pamper and spoil them, showering them with gifts they don't even need. On the other hand, women who respond with a bland "thanks," or a mere "oh, how nice," do nothing to encourage the man's generosity and therefore rob him of the joy of giving. Worse, some complain that the gift is not good enough, not right or not expensive enough.

Men have often worked hard to cater to the whims of femininity and have not only loved doing it but loved the women more because of it.

I have been speaking here of eagerness shown when a man gives a woman rather modest gifts and does small favors for her. In contrast to this, if a man should give her something of unusual value, or which requires sacrifice on his part, childlike joy could be inappropriate for such a momentous occasion. A deeply expressed appreciation may be more significant and rewarding to a man.

Another thing which every woman should know about giving is that when a man gives her something that she does not particularly like, or may even dislike, she should not make the big mistake of showing disappointment. A moment like this does not need to pose a problem, however, as many women would imagine. You need not force yourself to be insincere and act as though you like the gift if you honestly do not.

The thing to do is to appreciate not the gift, but the act of giving and the man giving it. Even your words can be carefully chosen to show appreciation for the man, for his thoughtfulness and his generosity. The gift is of little consequence in comparison to the man, his feelings and the beautiful moment which you may remember for a long time if you handle it wisely. Whatever the gift is, be sure to use it, or wear it if possible, at least for a while, with the deepest appreciation for the generous giver.

Men aren't always good at selecting things for women and are not likely to remember hints. When you aren't married, you don't really have a right to expect too much unless you have an understanding. Do not attach too much importance to this negligence or interpret it as a lack of caring for you.
Outspokenness

One of the best methods of displaying a childlike manner is in being outspoken. I do not wish to imply that we speak too frankly, with little concern for the feelings of others. The childlike manner I refer to is one of being direct in conversation, and not evasive, making excuses and failing to come to the point.

A little child who has been reared by kind and loving parents of whom he is not afraid tends to be honest and outspoken. He says such things as "I don't want to," or "oh, I forgot." For example, if you ask a little girl if she would like to go with you to visit Mrs. Grumbly down the street and the child really does not want to go, she might say "I don't want to." She does not hunt for excuses or ask to put it off until another time, etc. She is honest and direct. This is the sort of response a man appreciates from a woman.

If you are shopping with a man and he suggests that you buy something you dislike, it is not necessary to explain your objections. Be honest and outspoken and say, "I really don't think I want this one or, do you mind if I look for something else?" This comment will not only relieve the situation but will be appreciated and less likely to insult his tastes than would an elaboration of your ideas.

I knew a married girl who had this charm of outspokenness. On the occasion that I remember, her husband and several other men had just announced plans to sail down the Colorado River on a raft. The girl, thinking the trip quite extravagant, especially since she had been going without some of the things she needed, said in a very girlish manner, "But, what about me? I need a new dress." The man looked up at her in surprised wonder and amusement. How much better was this outspoken response than if she had tried to convince him of his selfishness, or even worse, had said nothing and held a grudge.

In some situations, a woman should encourage such manly plans with eagerness and excitement, but in her case the trip was really beyond their means, and her outspoken words brought him back to reality and kept her from feeling resentful about it. Since she felt she must express herself — it was wise to do so in a girlish and outspoken manner.

How to Ask for Things

Another art of childlikeness is knowing how to ask a man for things. I refer to things you want to have, to do, someplace you want to go, or something you want done for you. Even when you aren't married yet, you might very well find yourself in a situation where you need to ask for help from the man you are with.

Getting a man to do these things for you in a charming way is an art worth knowing, and so simple you would hardly believe it. A woman should never use any other approach with men.

We copy this art again from innocent little children. They just ask for things. They do not justify, explain or argue a point, for they are too dependent and incapable in the presence of adults. A little girl, when she wants something, might approach her father trustfully, realizing that he has the power to say yes or no. She will say "May I, please," or "Will you please," displaying her girlish attitude and causing her father to feel big and masculine, in the position of the leader. Soft hearted parents are bound to say yes to such childlike requests.

If you approach a man with a childlike request it gives him the feeling of validation, and therefore manliness. Not only will he be encouraged to help, but he will feel your childlike need, your littleness, in his manly position. He will enjoy doing things for you, catering to you and waiting upon you because of the wonderful way it makes him feel. If you do it right, he will jump at the chance to do things for you and will love you more because of it.

In asking a man for things, avoid these mistaken approaches:

1. Hinting. Men rarely get hints. They seldom remember these tip-offs from one day to the next. Men prefer a more direct approach. It's a relief for them. Understanding this can be a relief for you.

2. Convincing. This is also unsuccessful, since it places the woman in a debating mode with the man. He may actually want to help but might say no automatically, just because this approach offends him though he may not realize it.

He often doesn't realize the reason he took such a stand. Trying to convince him of anything using only logic might invite opposition and does nothing for the man's feeling manliness.

3. Demanding. This also doesn't work. A stubborn, argumentative attitude is distasteful, unattractive, and robs him of any feeling or desire to assist her.

The best method of asking a man for things is childlikeness, since it places a man in the proper position of protector and encourages him to say "yes." This in turn leads to a better relationship, since he feels more tenderly towards a woman he can serve. He is charmed by her little girlish requests which make him feel so much like a man.

In developing this art, be simple and direct and avoid such expressions as "let's do this," or "I think it would be nice if we were to do this," or other such suggestions.

Remember, there are a few things which you should not ask for. Do not ask for things which are selfish, or things which he cannot afford. Do not ask for love or tenderness. They are only of value when they are given voluntarily and lose their value when demanded under obligation. Also, avoid asking a man for a dance or a date unless it is "girl's choice," since this is much too aggressive for a feminine woman.

If a man says "no" to your request, do not be alarmed. Let it go.

Practice this art of asking for things with your father and any brothers and you will see for yourself their immediate response to your childlike request. Use this method when you need them to lift a heavy bundle, or move some furniture, or take you shopping, or help you with your homework or whatever.

Not only will they willingly oblige, but you will notice growing warmth in your relationship, for they will love you more as they do things for you. Be sure to always thank them in a most appreciative and girlish manner. Use this feminine psychology on all men in your life. They will delight in catering to your innocent whims and caprices and will not be able to resist the charms of such girlish femininity.

Childlike Manner

The childlike manner is the motions or actions of a woman which appear in her voice, facial expressions, or any other motions of the body. Dora had a charming childlike manner. Her delightful little voice and her dear little ways were not only feminine but childlike. At times she would shake her curls and point her finger at her little dog as little girls do. (If you don't have curls, don't worry about it. You can still get the idea).

David describes her childlike manner in his following observation: "By and by she made tea for us, which was so pretty to see her do, as if she was busying herself with a set of doll's things, that I was not particular about the quality of the beverage."

If you will watch little girls as they play house you will observe many things about childlike manner. They do not hurry through their chores "just to get them over with" as grown women sometimes do. They play house for the sheer joy of doing it. They sweep, cook, or tend the baby in a most unhurried and happy manner. A girlish woman will copy this same childlike manner in doing her housework or any work before her. She will delight in hanging up curtains, cooking a favorite recipe, cleaning out cupboards or even polishing floors. She does the same thing at a job or school. By so doing she demonstrates the inborn domestic nature found in little girls and so sadly missing in some adult women who rush through her work just to get it over with and heaves a sigh of relief when it is finished.

In The Cloister and the Hearth, you will remember that Margaret tied Gerard's ribbons in this same unhurried and girlish manner. Then the author comments, "It is not natural to her sex to hurry ought that pertains to the sacred toilet."

Girlish Trust

Still another trait of childlikeness is an attitude of trust. Just as a little girl respects her father as her leader and trusts his ability to take care of her, to provide for her, to solve problems and make wise decisions, a woman can show this same trust in a man she has a serious relationship with. This does not mean that she never expresses her-self in these matters or that she never warns him of difficulty or danger that she may perceive, but it does mean that she is extremely careful not to doubt his ability or capabilities. When it comes to a man, "let him figure it out" should be the rule. She should not, for example, tell him what to do. There is nothing a man dislikes more than a woman who gives him directions or instructions in things he feels he knows more about than she does.

I remember being in the company of a man and his fiancé who were trying to show us around the city they lived in. With every turn he made, she was there at his elbow telling him what to do and what not to do. Never make the mistake of telling a man where to turn unless he asks. It is better to let him make a million mistakes than to give him the feeling that you doubt his ability. Especially is this irritating in something as simple as finding his way around in life.

Never doubt a man's ability to solve a problem. For example, do not doubt his ability to fix a stalled car by suggesting that he call a repair man. He can think of that. Or do not doubt his ability to find his way out of a financial problem or other perplexing situation; or do not doubt his ability to reach difficult goals, such as achieving a high education or advancement in a job. To doubt his ability is to show a lack of trust.

On the other hand, if a man is trying to reach some difficult goal or solve a difficult problem, do not give him the impression that you expect it will be easy. For example, if a man intends to go through a difficult and long education, do not doubt his ability to reach his goal, but on the other hand, do not give an indication that you expect it will be easy and thereby rob him of his potential heroism. What a man wants is for you to recognize the difficulties of his goals and his problems but have a girlish trust that he will one way or another be victorious and that only a superior man such as he could do it. In this way you recognize opportunity for heroism and do not doubt his ability to be a hero. This is girlish trust.

Childlike Appearance

The last quality of childlikeness is that of appearance, in your clothes, grooming and also in your manner. The main thing to avoid is a mannish look. Also avoid matronly hair styles that are old fashioned and out of date. Young women should try to keep up with current hair styles. Doing so is an indication of femininity and girlishness.

Whatever you do, do not take on a masculine look in either your appearance or your manner. Always emphasize the differences between you and men. If you wear an item of clothing that is masculine inspired, pair it with something or some color that is decidedly feminine or something most men would not wear.

Childishness

Childlikeness should not be confused with "childishness," which is an immature quality. To be childish is to copy the faults of children, whereas to be childlike is to copy their virtues. Some unattractive traits children often have are self-centeredness, a lack of responsibility for their own actions, and expecting too much of ordinary human beings. Those who retain these traits in adult life tend to fret when they do not get their way, blame others for their unfortunate circumstances, fail to acknowledge their own mistakes and failures, and make unreasonable demands of their associates.

When we were young we expected much from our parents and thought they could do most anything. To project this unrealistic thought into adult life is to expect too much from our associates and therefore is childish. Childishness in a grown woman is unattractive to men and can even be offensive.

There are some women who resist the idea of acting childlike, who consider it an insult to their good sense to expect them to stomp their feet and shake their heads and to act the part of a little girl. They insist upon believing that really sensible men, the kind of man they want, would be repulsed instead of attracted to such a childlike creature. Even when these women agree that such a woman is the most attractive, they mistakenly assume that for them, the acting of such a part is ridiculous. Shaking your head and stomping your feet is only one suggestion. There are many childlike ways of responding and at least one or two that will fit perfectly for you.

Be assured that we all have this trait somewhere in our nature — it is a part of being feminine. Remember that it was not long ago that you were a little girl and all of these traits came naturally. You can recapture this manner, this charm, and make it a part of you again. You will be more fascinating to men and will make them feel bigger and manlier in your presence. This marvelous feeling is what makes childlikeness so fascinating to them.

Remember, if you want to be loved and cherished like a woman, you must make him feel like a man. There is a tendency when some women mature, to lose this childlike trait, especially after she gets married. She somehow feels that she must "grow up," without realizing that men never want women to lose this most adorable trait. Truly fascinating women always retain some childlike qualities, regardless of their age. They never take on unattractive and manly trait, nor do they become skeptical, stubborn, cynical and overbearing as some older women do who have lost their girlishness.

Summary of Angela Human

You now have a better picture of what a man finds ideal in a woman. There may be other traits that men find charming, but these are the most important. These are the ones that arouse his feelings of admiration and love and cause him to be fascinated, amused and enchanted while awakening in him a desire to protect and shelter.

You do not have to be all of these things at the same time. In fact, changefulness is charming in a woman. One time you should be bright and joyful, another time gentle and feminine, and another time saucy. Sometimes you will need to be serious, especially in your sympathetic understanding; but at other times have the giddiness, vivacity and teasing playfulness of a child, and occasionally an air of bewitching languor, or the kittenish or cooing quality which I described in the feminine manner.

If a man is cross, stern or overly serious, respond with teasing playfulness. If he neglects you and you have a feeling of being walked on or treated unfairly, respond with childlike sauciness. Any one of these approaches would be tiresome to a man if it the only response she has. He enjoys change, and you become more interesting and fascinating if you are unpredictable. As the author Charles Reade comments, "Girls like to be coy and tender, saucy and gentle by turns."

In your efforts to be fascinating do not neglect the Angelic side, which is just as essential as the Human in winning a man's love. Your admirable character, your ability to be a domestic goddess, especially after marriage, and your deep understanding of him and his problems balance the human side of you and make you more ideal. And remember, there is no single action as important as "accepting a man at face value" and allowing him to be himself. Other traits you might neglect, and he may still be attentive, but if you do not accept him he will not love you the way you need to be loved. You cannot turn aside from this essential ingredient to love. All else will fail without it.

In trying to attain the qualities of Angela Human, make a chart similar to the one in this book and keep it in a secret place. Then take one quality at a time, study it and practice for a week or so. During this time, notice men's reactions to your efforts.

It will be interesting to note how differently a man reacts when you concentrate on a specific quality than he does when you apply another. This is because you arouse in him a particular sentiment or another. Some things will amuse him, some will fascinate him and others will arouse a feeling of deep romantic love. When you have covered the subject, refer to the chart occasionally to keep on the track.

Rewards you can expect immediately. Men will notice you and be more attentive and interested. The results will probably seem unbelievable. You will be enjoying "flowers" instead of "weeds" and will never want to return to your former self again.

You may back-slide occasionally, but this should not discourage you. Always be renewed and make another effort. It takes about a year to form habits of lasting value. But if you will keep the goal clearly in mind and try to picture yourself as the ideal woman, you will advance to higher goals and will eventually become more of an Angela Human, never again to "eat the crumbs."

Making You Distinctly You

We have just covered in these chapters the essentials of feminine charm, the qualities that all women should strive for if they are to be attractive to men. However, we must take into consideration the fact that each person born on the earth has a unique personality. Each one of us has characteristics which set us apart from every other person, making us a distinct and different individual.

To reach our highest potential in charm, we build the basic structure of Angela Human and then add to it the crowning glory of our own unique personality. One thing which will greatly interfere with the unfolding of your own personality is to make the mistake of copying others too closely. Since they often have not yet completely discovered themselves, they look around for someone they find attractive and use her as a model to pattern after. If they copy goodness and femininity this is fine, but if they try to copy individualism, it will be like wearing a dress that does not fit.

I have had many young men tell me that one thing they admire in girls is genuineness and sincerity, and they are repelled by girls who try to be too much like someone else. Instead of wasting your time trying to copy someone else's charm, try to discover the real self you were born to be and work to polish it up to its brightest.

Begin to build your own personality. Deliberately avoid being like someone else. After a while you will turn inward for ideas and will soon find an unlimited supply. There are sometimes a few barriers to the unfolding of a charming personality.

They come in the form of shyness, low self-esteem and the lack of social ease around men.

The next chapter will be devoted to a study of these problems and suggestions for gaining confidence with men.

Confidence, or Social Ease with Men

One of the keys to a charming personality is an air of confidence. If you will observe girls who are fascinating, you will notice that they are self-assured around men. They are at ease with them and therefore men are at ease around them. Confidence is essential to feminine charm, whereas shyness can be a problem.

In learning to acquire this asset of personality, remember: Few are as confident as they appear to be. Most of us have a few insecurities and find he need from time to time to put on a front of confidence to a degree.

But by acting confident we give others a feeling of ease, and by doing this, our confidence will naturally grow. Acquiring the attributes of Angela Human will also build confidence. The art and charm of femininity will result in more confidence.

Don't Be A Wallflower

Social affairs, especially dances in which boys and girls are invited to attend without dates, "can present the painful problem to girls who aren't often asked to dance. This is what is called being a "wallflower". Being left on the sidelines will do nothing for a girl but weaken her confidence around men. Don't allow yourself to be placed in this humiliating, degrading position.

If you should find yourself in this unfortunate situation, leave the dance and go into the corridor and walk around for a while, then return. Do not be seen either sitting or standing on the sidelines. If you are repeatedly left out, you are practicing the art of feminine charm can change your whole world.

Build Confidence By a Good Appearance

One of the best ways to build confidence is to always look your best. Never permit yourself to appear at a disadvantage — to be handicapped by a slovenly hairdo, dowdy clothing or unclean body.

Take better care of yourself, learn to sew if necessary and learn the art of make-up and hair styles until you have achieved an appearance that will impress others favorably and build better confidence in yourself.

One of the advantages of a charming appearance is not so much what it does to others as what it does to the girl herself, and the social grace and confidence she acquires along with it. When she "feels pretty" she also feels confident.

Overcoming an Inferiority Complex

A feeling of inferiority around friends and associates can undermine confidence and in turn detract from your feminine charm. There can be any number of things that cause this feeling. Less money, less education, or fewer nice clothes can make a girl feel unequal. Or she may not feel as pretty, or that she has the same adequate social background. She may feel that other people have talents or achievements that far outshine hers. These things cause a feeling of inadequacy around people who may appear to have these advantages.

You need not have any special advantage or talent to feel equal to everyone you meet. In the most cultured society we meet people with the most charming personalities who have no particular accomplishments except their own selves to offer.

These people will applaud the accomplishments of the orator, the financier, the artist, the poet, and geniuses of every description, yet they do not themselves think, nor does anyone else think, that they are inferior to those whom they applaud. Their own self-assurance has made them appear equal to every other person. We can do the same by acquiring an "air of confidence."

1. Lack of Talents and Accomplishments. If you feel inadequate around certain people because they may have developed some talent which you have not, it is important that you have a good attitude towards yourself and also towards the other person. Just because he or she has chosen to concentrate dedicated efforts in a particular direction does not mean that this person is superior. You are just as valuable. You were born with beautiful eyes, ears and all parts of your body. You are a child of God, with the potentials this concept embraces. You may not have developed your abilities and talents to the same degree, but you are no less precious. You could be just as much of a shining light if you chose to work for those goals.

When you are in the presence of someone whom you think is more talented, say to yourself, "Just because she has done things I have not is no reason for thinking she is a better person than I am. I have not chosen to put my efforts in that direction. I am sure that if I did choose to develop my talents as she has done, and if I tried hard enough and long enough, I would prove talented also.

For example, don't imagine, if you happen to meet an author, that you are inferior to him because you have never been able to write anything. If you had worked as hard as he has, written and destroyed as many miserable attempts at writing as he, you would very likely be able to do as well as he. If you have not chosen to use your time in such pursuits that is no reason for believing that the author is any better than yourself. The same is true with anyone whose talents and accomplishments shine brightly before you. Recognize their efforts as worthy of appreciation, but do not underestimate your own worth.

2. Lack of Money and Material Wealth. If you are a person who is lacking in material possessions, and if you associate with people who have far more, you may have a feeling of inferiority in their presence. Your biggest thought, perhaps, is that others will depreciate you because of your lack. There are many fine people who have no money to speak of, who do not have this attitude at all.

Most people are more sensitive to your lack of self-assurance than your lack of funds. If you did not think of your poverty and let it affect your manner and self-assurance, the fact that you are not fortunate financially would seldom cross their minds. But even if it should, they are attracted to the fine character and sparking personality that you are and admire you even more because you have achieved it without the support of money. If you will put aside your poverty as a thing not worth thinking about, others will likely do same.

In some cases, money is earned by great and dedicated effort, just as in any other notable accomplishment. If this is so, then you can admire the person for that effort which was all focused in one direction, but not for the wealth itself.

In comparing yourself with people of means, do not consider merely the possession of wealth as admirable, but the way in which it is used. That is the only way to measure values. If you meet someone who uses money in a noble, honorable, generous or artistic way, then give that person the special honor due him. It is how the money is used or the character of the individual that commands our respect.

3. Lack of Expensive Clothes. Sometimes it is not merely the absence of wealth which causes self-consciousness, but the absence of fine clothes such as our wealthier associates wear. In some circles cliques are formed in which it appears that expensive clothes are the factors governing admission. In reality, however, what excludes many a girl is not the inferiority of her clothing, but the air of being so acutely and painfully aware of her lack that, regardless of her clothes, she is not good company. She is so uncomfortable because of her imaginary disadvantage that she casts a damper on the spirits of her companions. She is not excluded because of her clothing, but because she seems odd or unpleasant. When girls and boys have a good time, they want a lively, interesting group; they

don't want anyone who thinks mostly of her lack of expensive apparel.

If this has been your problem, forget your clothes and talk to these people as if your clothes were as good as theirs. Just because your clothes are not expensive does not mean, that you cannot be attractive — and just as attractive as those persons who wear costly designer apparel. A charm teacher explained to me that women of money are not always impeccably dressed, whereas other women of less means who will study and learn the art of dressing attractively, choosing clothing becoming to them, can outshine women with money, and often do. If you cannot afford attractive clothes, you could learn to sew with skill and learn the art of copying expensive designs. In this way you can compete with most women — even on a limited budget.

4. Lack of Education. Many young women have opportunity for education. Take advantage of these schools of learning, both for the knowledge they bring to life and for the feeling of confidence an education brings. If you do feel inferior to your associates because you do not appear as well educated as they, then work a little harder and take advantage of any educational institutions available. Remember, however, as you go through life, that it is the application of knowledge that counts. Learning just a few facts is of no particular value in building confidence. The application of these facts is.

Remember also that education in itself will not make you fascinating to men, but the confidence that an education builds will.

5. Lack of Social Prestige. When you meet with people whom you consider highly polished, being yourself, perhaps, rather awkward and sheepish in such company, don't believe that these polished socialites are any better than you are. Never imagine that you are not as good as anyone else with whom you come in contact; never let yourself be deferential or be made to feel inferior.

It is important for a girl to feel equal to her associates if she is to have the social ease necessary for real charm. It is difficult for a girl to radiate charm or to be fascinating to a man she feels inferior to. Her own unique and charming personality will be smothered by her withdrawn and under confident manner and attitude. She need not feel inferior, however, to a particular man, or to anyone.

We have learned that the way to social ease is to acquire an air of confidence. Still another way to confidence is by developing the art of conversation. Those tense moments when we can't think of anything to say can make us feel ill at ease around people. Developing this art will promote confidence, making not only yourself, but everyone else feel at ease. This is not a difficult art to acquire. The following are some suggestions.

How to Be a Good Conversationalist

Have you ever found yourself ill at ease in a group because you have never learned the art of conversation? The talk turns to music, art, travel or baseball, fishing or social activities, and you can't think of a single thing to say. Or you meet an attractive man for the first time. You feel as if you were tongue-tied.

The best way to overcome this feeling is to listen carefully to the person you are with.

Being A Conversationalist Star

1. Background Information. Ask him questions. Where is he from? What are his interests? Men and also women love others who are interested in them and what they think.

2. Practice. Take every opportunity to engage in conversation with many types of people. Be interested in them, who they are and what they are interested in. You will get better the more you practice this.

3. Let the Other Person Talk. Encourage the other person to talk about himself, since this is at least half of the art of good conversation. Begin by making some comment or suggestion which will lead him to talk. Ask leading questions, but do not ask pointed questions, or ones that can be answered with yes or no. If the conversation lags, then you can begin drawing from your own store of ideas. Try to talk only a minute or so about yourself and give the other person a chance to make comments.

4. Dating: On dates, be sure to carry your share of the conversation and do not expect your partner to do it all, unless he seems to want to. Double and triple dates make conversation easier, since everyone present can make a contribution and seem more at ease and usually more talkative.

You can also learn the art of conversation on these double dates, by listening to your friends.

Things to Avoid in Conversation

Don't gossip, use sarcasm, embarrass anyone, hurt or belittle anyone. Don't brag, talk about yourself too much, or over-use the word "I".

When someone is talking don't swing the conversation to focus on you. Don't interrupt or pry into people's private affairs. Don't say, "I know a better one than that" and thus deflate the other person's story.

Please don't swear, use profanity, slang, coarse language, or vulgar stories.

Lose Self-Centeredness

Another way to social ease is work on self-centeredness. Try to avoid thinking mostly about yourself, how you look, what others are thinking of you, whether they like you or not, if they think you are pretty, etc. An over-concern about your own defects will cause you to feel ill at ease around people.

Although a good appearance is important in making a proper impression, most men will certainly not notice a few flaws. They will be more interested in your charming manner and your interest in them. Always dress carefully and groom yourself; but once you arrive in public, it is useless to continue to think of your appearance. Overcome this defect by trying to become genuinely interested in others, and practice forgetting about yourself for a while. In learning the way to social ease, remember the following essential points in this chapter:

1. Take on an air of confidence.

2. Try to not do things which destroy confidence.

3. Have a good appearance.

4. Become a good conversationalist.

5. Practice the art of not focusing on you.

Part 2
Strategy with Men

Introduction

Do not let the word strategy alarm you. It is a perfectly legitimate word for our subject. Why shouldn't a girl use strategy with men? After all, her charms, her feminine wiles and ways are the primary means she has of winning the attention of men, from whom she will choose her lifetime partner.

Isn't it right, then, that she knows everything that she can about men and use every strategy possible to win their attention and interest?

Part one has been devoted to helping you become the kind of girl a man wants. You must have something to offer if you are to win the attention of good men. We have also covered the little feminine wiles and ways that enhance her so that she becomes an enchanting and fascinating creature. If you have taken these chapters to heart and have applied them, you have no doubt gone far towards making yourself a womanlier woman, a bundle of feminine charm, girlish and tender in manner and general impression. Altogether you will be, if this progress is maintained, a girl any man might be attracted to, a girl well worth his attention and interest.

However, you do not want to win just any man, but one particular man. The one perfect for you. One day when you least expect it, you may chance to meet this special man, the one who will have everything you have ever wanted. But you may find the perplexing problem of being faced with competition. He may have numerous other girls in whom he is interested. Or he may be lost in the pursuit of a career, so that although you are a fascinating girl, and meet every specification he may have in mind for a wife, he may not take you seriously. With such difficulties staring you in the face, you will need to have a thorough knowledge of men. You will need to have every charm, tactic and strategy at your command to win this one rare gem of manhood.

You are now ready to begin the study of winning the man of your dreams, first in being directed to the right kind of man and second in knowing how to awaken his interest and desire and third in removing the obstacles that may stand in the way of marriage.

This is the division of study upon which we will now concentrate.

Chapter 18

Where and How to Meet Men

Where Most Men Are Available

In our modern times the most available places to meet men are on our college campuses, which are filled with ambitious manhood. Some colleges are predominantly male, others more nearly equal, and a few predominantly female. Next to college campuses, the armed services provide the largest numbers of men. Their bases are scattered across the country. Here, however, you would have to be particular and selective.

The army inducts men of all types and levels. But, although some would not be of your caliber, others are the very cream of manhood. One can take care to associate only with a man of good character. Industries also hire large numbers of young men, and these are also scattered across the country. Those industries that hire large numbers of men and only a few women might be a good choice.

One of the best places to meet men is in church. Churches provide a friendly atmosphere, and almost always a newcomer is introduced, seldom overlooked. Churches are also interested in the welfare of young people and usually provide social activities where men and women can meet properly. To meet your men friends, and eventually your mate, from among people who have the same or similar religious views is the most ideal selection for future happiness and harmony in the home. Perhaps you think that men don't go to church, at least young men; but that does not mean that their mothers and their sisters and girlfriends and their cousins don't. Become so well acquainted with them that you will be invited to their homes and their social events. Thus, you may gain the acquaintanceship of the masculine side of the family. Churches in some cities, however, especially small cities and towns, are depleted of available men in our modem times. Many of them have gone to larger cities to attend college or find employment or have joined the armed services.

If you are an eligible young woman and are in an environment with a limited opportunity to meet men, it may be wise to consider a change if possible. This is not to say that you will necessarily meet your future mate from among large numbers. You may possibly meet him while traveling on the airplane, or at some small party. But your chances are less likely in a limited field.

It is important that you widen your opportunities to meet men if you have few in your social group. Remember, meeting men and eventually your lifetime partner is the most important step, even the most important decision you make. Use every means available to you, make every plan necessary to provide yourself with the widest and finest opportunity to meet good men.

The Best Opportunities to Meet Men

Your friends and associates provide the best opportunities to meet men. It is through them that you are invited to parties, socials, outings, or are introduced individually to many potential partners. Did it ever occur to you what a wide opportunity you have to meet many men through building a large circle of friends and associates? The young man you may someday marry will most likely be met through one of these friends, and perhaps through one you may least expect would do you such a favor.

Since your friends and acquaintances could be of importance in your strategy with men, the first thing to do is to increase the number of them. Though some may not become your best friends, you can at least promote a casual friendship. Networking is valuable on many levels.

Girlfriends

Girlfriends can be your greatest allies. Increase your number of intimate girlfriends to include as many as you possibly have time for. All true friendships require time and attention. They will invite you to their parties and introduce you to men they know, and even to other girls. Do not stop with just your circle of intimate girlfriends. Acquire a wide number of acquaintances. You can be friendly to the girl you sit next to in class, or pass each day on the way to lunch, or see in the grocery store. The more of these you have the better.

Although you will have more than one reason for your many friends, this does not mean that your friendships must be insincere. Once you have made a friendship or acquaintance, make it a genuine one, and be a true and loyal friend.

Every girl can be lovely and charming. It is neither physical beauty nor money nor expensive clothing that creates the illusion of fascinating charm that will begin to win men's hearts. Every girl can acquire it.

In using feminine charm with men, be everything that a woman should be, and then choose friends and associates who will not detract from that picture but rather add to it.

Male Friends

Widen your circle of male friends just as you do your circle of girlfriends, but when it comes to dating, choose only men whom you consider as a spouse if possible. Remember, you will marry someone you date. Take care to try to date only good men. You won't be perfect of course. But do the best you can.

It is not necessary to date only men whom you find the most attractive. A man whom you think you could never possibly become interested, but who is a man of character, could nevertheless make a good escort to take you to important social occasions. Simply going out with him does not obligate you to marry him. If the man takes pleasure in your company, that pleasure is its own reward, provided you don't lead him on with false hopes.

You never know. You might fall in love with him in the process.

Your friendship could be a social convenience to both of you, providing an opportunity for both to meet a wider circle of acquaintances.

You do not owe it to anyone to date them. They can be turned down gently and kindly. Simply say, "I'm sorry, I am going to be busy tonight." If he should lack the manners to accept such a brief refusal and ask "why?," you do not owe him any explanation. Just repeat the original statement by saying "I have some things to do." If you do turn down a date with a young man, do not make the mistake of accepting another date for the same evening. This is not kind and is also dishonest.

Older Friends and Children

Do not limit your friendships to people of your own age. You can be casual friends with anyone of any age. To become friends with the older people is to enrich your life with their special experiences and contacts. Older people have many friends and contacts. Children, also, can lead you to a wide circle of boys and girls your own age.

Take the little girl next door, for instance. You may never have thought of paying any unusual attention to her, but she may have an eligible young uncle or cousin, or her playmate may have a big brother, or either of them may have a handsome, single family member with whom you may become acquainted someday. Similarly, with every man, woman and child you know — all of them may have relatives or friends unknown to you now, whom you may someday be desirous of meeting. The narrower your circle of friends, the fewer men you are likely to meet and the less likelihood of your meeting the right one. The broader your acquaintances, the more men you are likely to meet and the more likelihood of your meeting the one destined for you.

Nor should you neglect a friendship merely because you see no present prospect of their helping you meet others. At any time, this acquaintance may have a visitor or acquire a new connection that will enable him or her to introduce you to someone who could be important in your life. It does not cost you anything to make a great number of acquaintances, and to keep on friendly terms with them is a good idea. You should be kind and loving to everyone.

Take Advantage of All Social Events & Where Eligible Good Men Are

You do not need to depend alone upon social events where you are invited. Of course, accept every invitation to attend these parties and events that you can. But you can also attend certain socials that are open to the public. In other words, if you are in college, go to the library at night —someone is sure to see you and might introduce you. Or attend the lecture series that the college offers, or the musical events and plays. You can attend these with girlfriends, and men are sure to be present. You will, of course, have to study a lot while in college. There is ample time in the college schedule for a girl to do both study and meet men. Attend every open affair you can, especially socials, for at such places it's easy to meet people. You can meet more men in one evening at a social or party than you would otherwise in a month.

Being a Good Hostess

You may further add to your skills by becoming a good hostess and planning some parties of your own. There is perhaps nothing that will more quickly make you popular with men and women alike than being a good hostess. If people enjoy themselves at your home or apartment and at your affairs, they will naturally avail themselves of your hospitality at every opportunity. This is particularly true with men.

Sometimes girls will go to a social which doesn't sound like fun because they are afraid of offending the hostess, who is likely a friend, by not coming. Not so with men; if they don't expect to have a good time, a team of horses, as a rule, cannot drag them to such an affair.

Helping people enjoy themselves requires some skill, but mostly caring for others. Make sure you have plenty of good food. Learning to cook is a great advantage here. Especially homemade! Decorations can be simple, if money is in short supply. The most important thing is to treat all your guests with genuine warmth, not just a particular man you hope to impress.

Don't Stay at Home

In reviewing our subject of how and where to meet men, we have stated that we first place ourselves, if possible, in an environment where many men are present — to give ourselves the greatest opportunity of numbers. Then we arrange to meet men through friends and increase our chances by increasing our circle of friends. We also attend every social event possible and every event where good men are present. And lastly, we create social events of our own by giving parties and outings, etc.

One last point is this. Don't stay home unless it is absolutely necessary. Every chance you have to go out must be taken advantage of. And if you do not have the opportunity to go places, then you can create such opportunities of your own.

For example, attend church on Sunday. In the afternoon ask a girl friend to go for a walk with you, and then find some excuse to call on another girl. You are likely to meet some new acquaintances during the day and old ones too. If you stay at home constantly you are likely to meet no one.

On other days, as well as holidays, take every opportunity to meet people, especially young men. Attend programs, fairs, exhibitions, games, sports of all kinds, parades, picnics, conventions, etc. Who knows just when and where you are going to meet the man who will be the love of your life?

A dancing class, a gym class, a night school, a class, gives you an opportunity to become acquainted with other people, and through them, their brothers and cousins and friends.

Chapter 19

Choosing a Mate

The most important decision you will make in life is to choose your partner in marriage, the man who will be the father of your children and your companion for a lifetime. Choose with care and seek to be guided by the greatest wisdom.

The most important guide you can ever have to assist you in the selection of your lifetime partner is found in prayer. Ask for guidance each and every day of your life. Pray for a mate who will be suitable, one with whom you can be joyously happy, and prepare yourself to be just as fine a companion for him. You are a child of God and are entitled to this special wisdom and guidance if you live worthy to receive it. He is interested in you and in your welfare and happiness. In addition to prayer, God will expect you to do the best you can. Work to gain wisdom and good sound judgment, and to develop a sense of values to assist you in finding a good man. The following suggestions are given for this purpose:

Set Your Goals High

Since marriage is a most important step, set your goals high. Your husband will be your day-in, day-out companion and the father of your children. He will set the scene which will be yours for the rest of your life; together you will make major decisions and determine the policies the family will follow. Choose as wisely as you can and aim for a man of great and true worth. This implies, of course, that you are a girl of equal worth, or are working to become one. It would hardly be fair to expect to find a special man if you do not also have something special to offer as a wife.

The trouble with some girls is that they do not know what true worth means in a man, or which different qualities join together to make up an admirable character and personality. And, if a girl already has in mind an image of the "ideal man" for her, she may not know how to go about discovering his character. How can she go about finding out if a man has he character she is looking for? Some guidelines are given in this chapter.

Try not to have preconceived ideas about a man's appearance, or outer shell, such as his color of eyes, hair, his build, how tall, etc. Although we all admire handsome men, to place this attribute as a requirement might blind us to some true values that last.

In my lifetime I have known a few girls who made this mistake. One was set on marrying a man with brown eyes. It was a very strange thing how blind this girl was due to one quirk in her thinking. She passed up at least three blue-eyed men who wanted to marry her and who would have, in my opinion, made excellent husbands. She finally married a man with brown eyes. He turned out to be a disappointment to her and everyone else. He was both abusive and lazy. There are certainly excellent men with every color of eyes, but to have this notion in your head when it comes to mate selection is a mistake.

A similar case was a girl who wanted to marry the most handsome man she could find. She told her girlfriends, "When I walk down the street I want everyone to say, 'What a lucky girl!'" True to her vow, she did marry an especially handsome man, as everyone had to admit, but it was not long until he began cheating on her and she was heartbroken.

Handsome men can, of course, be as worthy as any others, but to place this feature on the list of requirements is to distort your perspective. Although beauty is a marvelous thing, we must discredit it in human relations, since it has little to do with love or happiness. You can fall in love with a good man, even if he doesn't appear especially attractive to you at first. He will look better and better to you as you know him.

An opposite case is a girl who, instead of having a weak sense of values, had about the highest standards in her estimation of manhood as can be imagined. The girl was young, beautiful and talented, but she married a man who was disabled in a wheelchair. When she announced her plans for marriage, her parents were grieved, and her friends astonished. In consoling them she explained, "This man has every quality I have ever wanted in a man. I will not let his physical handicap blind me to his true worth."

Here was a girl of fine character and values. Although this case is extreme and unusual, there are some lessons to be learned from it. Some girls make the mistake of limiting their choice to a man who is popular or much sought after by all the girls.

These shining socialites may, or may not, make good husbands. And although we must acknowledge that a man who has is especially charming is appreciated by us all, we must discredit
his popularity as being any specific advantage in being an ideal mate.

Another mistake is to give so much credit to social etiquette and propriety that it blinds you to other more important character traits. Certainly, these are admirable traits, but they should not be a determining factor in selecting a companion.

A woman of my acquaintance confided to me that many years before she had broken up with a young man because he did not use his butter knife during dinner. As it turned out, he was a wonderful man and outstanding in his field.

Neither the handsome man, the popular socialite, nor the men of propriety are necessarily desirable as mates unless they also possess the qualities of true worth. And I might add, neither is the football hero, the "life of the party" or the man who wins the medals, the trophies or the awards. These men may or may not make excellent husbands.

In any event, these outer signs are not those that count; they are not the real values. You will have to search for the "diamonds" in manhood. They may not be the glowing young men of the moment, but one might be perfect for you. Men aren't fully developed to their potential at this stage in life anyway.

The men of great worth may not be easy to find or to recognize. There is an old song which expresses this viewpoint impressively:

My Ideal

(The word girl has been changed to "boy.")

Will I ever find the boy in my mind,
The one who is my ideal?
Will I ever see the one who might be
Just around the comer waiting for me?
Will I recognize the light in his eyes
That no other eyes reveal,
Or will I pass him by and never even know
That he is my ideal?

~ Chet Baker

What to Look For

Look for traits of character in men. Look for dependability, honesty, loyalty, idealism, fairness and courage. Look for intelligence and also resourcefulness (the ability to solve problems). Then look for tenderness, thoughtfulness and kindness.

An ideal man is part steel and part velvet. He has the strong unbendable traits of steadfastness and unyielding determination, but also the velvet traits of gentle tenderness. This makes a real manly man.

In addition to the traits of character, look for his masculine traits. Remember the role of man, that he was born to be the guide, protector and provider for his family. A worthy mate will have strong leadership ability and be planning to provide for his family. He will be protective of you in times of danger or cold and will offer his masculine assistance when you are in need. For example, he will offer to lift heavy objects for you and protect you, etc.

This, of course, is assuming you are living the principles of femininity. Although a strong body build is admirable, and women can't help but appreciate it, it would be a mistake to put so much emphasis upon this trait that you fail to see other qualities in him. The masculine characteristics of aggressiveness and determination count for even more.

You will have to get to know him if you are to discover his masculine and character traits. Spend many hours with him. Lead him into conversations which will reveal his attitudes about responsibilities, about family life and about his future. Find out how he feels about religion, children and money. What are his attitudes about material things? Does he tend to concentrate mostly on material comforts and pleasures, or does he value the things of real worth? Is he ambitious or is he lazy and expects to be taken care of by you?

Although we should not have aims that are unrealistic and cannot expect to find a man without any weaknesses, we do need to be aware of true values and appreciate them.

Some Men to Avoid

There are definitely some men to avoid. One is a man of weak character. If you are considering a man who is inclined to be dishonest, lazy or weak, who has no moral convictions, then you are treading on dangerous ground. Also avoid men who have serious bad habits like excessive drinking, or promiscuity with women. Another problem is a man who is abusive in any way. Most girls would naturally try to avoid these types of men, but it is possible to be fooled.

It is surprising to see women whom we would assume to choose wisely who use the poorest of judgment in selecting a mate. They too often let their hearts rule logic. The fact that these men can and sometimes do overcome their bad habits is not worth the risk for the girl involved.

Another thing to watch for is a man with a giant ego. This is the man who must have the conversation always focused on himself, his accomplishments, skills and abilities, etc. A tendency to this once in a while may be normal in many men, but an excess may be a sign of insecurities which may spell trouble later. This does not mean that you should not consider him as a possibility, since a woman can often successfully help a man to overcome this insecurity by her understanding and confidence.

Sometimes a man may have suffered from a lack of appreciation during his youth. You may just be the one who, through believing in him, helps to bring out his true greatness. You should, however, be aware of these problems.

Some Facts to Face

As we learned in an earlier chapter, when you marry you must be willing to accept a man at face value. You cannot hope (nor should you) to remake him into some preconceived image you may have in mind. You wouldn't want him to do that to you. You will have to accept him, his faults, his weaknesses, his religion or lack of it, his ideas and standards as they are. You will be in for trouble if you enter marriage with the thought of changing a man to meet your specifications.

Not only will your efforts be fruitless, but they may prove to be a wedge in your home life that can be disheartening. So, face the fact that you must accept him as he is.

Along with this, you cannot expect to extract promises from him to make changes in his behavior after marriage. This is unfair and doesn't work.

Each person must retain his choice between good and bad and no other individual has a right to try to force a change. You cannot expect him to promise that he will drop a certain bad habit, or attend church regularly, etc.

Also, you cannot expect him to promise that he will live in a particular town, or associate only with certain types of people, or promise that he will reach a certain goal. A man is happy only when he feels accepted as he is.

With these thoughts in mind, you can see that it pays to take serious thought of the man he is now. Can you accept him as he is? Can you be happy with him with no changes? These are things to carefully consider.

233

Physical Affection During Dating

A young woman who wants a man of real worth has many factors to consider, as is plain to see. She must search for traits of character and masculine characteristics. She must also not be blind to a man's weaknesses. Add to this the tremendous importance of the decision — the outcome in the future if the choice is foolish and the rewards if the choice is wise — and one can begin to feel the responsibility involved in making this important choice.

It is wise, therefore, to not become involved in physical affection while these conclusions are being reached. When passions are stirred the mind is not entirely reliable. One can compare it to the effect of alcohol on the mind. We all know that when a person is drunk his reasoning is not dependable. A wises person would not think of making a momentous decision while under the effects of an alcoholic beverage.

The same is true with considering a companion — one would be foolish to select a lifetime partner while passions are aroused, and sensibilities therefore compromised. For this reason, more than any other, it is extremely foolish to indulge in too much physical affection before these important decisions have been reached.

Still another reason to avoid physical intimacy during mate selection is that a young woman will need many hours to get acquainted. She will need time to get to really know him. When they become passionate too soon, their time is consumed in this practice and they are robbed of the valuable time they need to learn about each other.

What Chance Do I Have of Winning the Man I Love?

Once you have found the man who meets every specification that you feel is essential, and your heart is set upon winning him, you will likely wonder what your chances are. If you have applied all of the principles of Fascinating Womanhood and have made progress towards the goal of Angela Human, then your chances are excellent indeed.

However, you may need to use a bit of strategy. All of the remainder of Part Two is devoted to a study of this subject and will teach you, step by step, how to learn what it takes to have the best chance to win his love.

There is one fact remaining that we must recognize. Just as you are drawn to certain types of men, so men will also be drawn to certain types of women—certain personalities. There is always a possibility that you will not be his type. This may be painful to face, but it need not make you unhappy. After all, you want a man who will appreciate you — the woman you really are — who will adore your personality as it is. You want a man who loves you.

It is heavenly to finally win a man who loves you for what you really are, and it would be misery to marry a man who could never appreciate the real you. Wait. Be patient until you find not only the man you can adore, but one who adores you also. If things do not work out with a particular man, in spite of all efforts, accept it as an answer to prayer and keep searching for the right man to come along.

Chapter 20

The 6 Stages of Attracting a Man

In learning how to attract a man who you would want to marry, it is important to look at these 6 important steps:

1. Be a girl worth having

2. Winning his attention

3. Gaining his interest

4. Creating desire

5. Overcoming hesitancy

6. Bringing to action

How Women Apply These Principles of Human Nature

These principles can be used with success by any young lady desiring to attract a man. Whether you are an orator seeking to win people to your cause, a dramatist seeking to win customers to your entertainment, a sales manager seeking to attract people to your market, or a young lady seeking to win the love of her life, these principles, when applied correctly and with the right motive, are effective. They are not the principles of oratory, drama, salesmanship or of courtship. They are really principles of human nature.

This does not mean that all young girls who attract the man they love understand the principals involved. Nature, which always intended that men and women should fall in love and marry, sometimes impels girls to follow unconsciously the same methods that the orator and sales manager would follow consciously. Such girls, who may sometimes be looked upon as nature's favorites, apparently need no other guidance but their impulses and instincts. They seem to always do the right thing at the right time and would seem to attract every man they meet.

Other girls, though not so universally attractive, have their latent instincts for attracting men aroused by meeting a particular man they are drawn to. They suddenly seem to blossom and show all evidence of real charm, to the surprise of everyone, including themselves. We all know of instances of such transformations.

But, as was stated in the introduction of this book, there is a vast army of girls, many of them both lovely and lovable, who cannot depend upon instincts in the matter of attracting men. Either through a habit of indifference to these instincts, or through an artificial culture that has made the suppression of their natural instincts habitual, they have permitted these natural instincts to grow rusty.

Even when nature does prompt them to do the right thing as far as attracting men is concerned, they hold back because of some learned distrust of their natural feminine impulses or a fear of appearing childish. Our culture often teaches women to disregard feminine instincts. As a result, these instincts can be distrusted to the point they must depend upon something more than womanly intuition for guidance in fascinating men.

But the absence of guiding instincts is no reason for discouragement. Many successful salesmen suffer in the beginning from the same handicap; yet it is universally acknowledged that the natural salesman who depends upon instinct cannot compete with the salesman who follows established principles. Nor can the born speaker achieve the heights of oratory to which the trained speaker can attain. Just as these mastered an accomplishment for which they first seemed to have no natural aptitude, so can seemingly uninteresting girls, by learning how to apply the principles of feminine human nature, make themselves masters of the art of captivating men, even when at first there seemed to be no remembered natural talent. The trained winner of men's hearts, through these principles, can attract men more than pretty girls who depend upon instinct alone.

Is Feminine Strategy Wrong or Unfeminine?

Do not think that the strategy or use of feminine principles of attracting men is in the least unrighteous or unfeminine. Is it not right that a young woman should become fascinating and adorable and deliberately plan to attract the attention of a good man? Is it not right that she should become a girl worth having and then try to inspire in some man's heart a desire for her? Her charm and her femininity are her primary tools in attracting men. Society does not assist her, other than to give her places to meet men. The girl stands alone, guided only by scattered knowledge, to win the man she will spend the rest of her life with. She must have some means of attracting a worthy man.

Remember, it is right that a girl marries and has a family. This is the main thing she wants, a little home of her own, a little nest to warm with her love and rule with her kindness. She wants merely to be someone's partner, to love him and share with him his joys and sorrows, to sustain the one and comfort the other, to climb with him towards higher and holier aspirations. She wants merely an opportunity to be tender, loyal and devoted.

She wants to avoid the lonely life of being unmarried, with no one to care for, to work for, to live for and die for. This is not unfeminine. It is the holiest design a woman can entertain. To use her charms, her feminine wiles and ways, and a plan based upon proven principles of human nature is fitting for her goals. It is not selfish for men hope to find a woman to adore too. The motive for a girl of character is the promotion of all involved.

The First Stage: Be A Girl Worth Having

The first part of the stages of winning men is to "be a girl worth having." Since all of Part One has been devoted to giving you a picture of such a girl, the kind of girl a man wants, we will only stress its importance here in our strategy in attracting good men.

Unless you are a girl with good character, one a good man is looking for, one who will confer a real benefit upon the man who marries her, you might indeed attract his attention or arouse his interest, but you are little likely to create in him a desire to marry you. If you do, you will both likely end up very unhappy.

You will want to work to acquire all of the qualities of Angela Human if you are to be a girl the man of your dreams will fit with. Here, too, a warning must be given. Many girls will skip the first part of the plan and concentrate upon the remaining five.

The latter ones, the application of the principles, are naturally the most interesting and seem the most practical part of the work. You may get the impression that with the many ingenious arts and devices outlined in the next five chapters for attracting a man, the mastery of the first part may seem of comparative insignificance. This is entirely wrong.

Unless you understand a man's ideal woman as outlined in Part One, unless you apply this viewpoint in making yourself more desirable, you will be much less likely to succeed.

If you expect to meet with the greatest chance of success, you will proceed through this work in the order given and not jump immediately to the last part, or more seemingly fun part of becoming a fascinating girl.

Winning a Man's Attention

or

How to Inspire Men to Notice You

We have just learned that the first step in attracting men is to be a girl worth having. But just as the salesman cannot depend upon his good product to sell itself, a young girl cannot rely upon her good character to get men to notice her.

We can learn from the tactics of the business world though it might sound strange. For example, what does the average commercial institution do when it has an exceptionally good article to offer the public? It advertises.

In many respects you are just like that manufacturer, except that you have something a hundred times better to offer — yourself, a girl worth having. But it doesn't matter how well worth having you are unless the right men know it.

Therefore, you will have to follow the example of the manufacturer — use every method consistent with a feminine woman to let good men know that you are alive, who you are, where you can be seen, and what you are worth. You want them to notice you and meet you and learn about you until they can appreciate your full value.

Some girls shrink from calling attention to themselves, and in consequence never meet men likely to be interested in them. Others are too bold, too obviously eager to get attention, and thereby risk cheapening themselves in some men's eyes.

First, you must not be content to sit at home every night. How will men be able to find you if you do? You may be the most desirable girl in the entire world but what good will it do you or anyone else if you hide yourself in your bedroom? You will have to get out in the world and circulate around men. Attend every social, sports event, church affair, cultural function, visit to the library, etc., that you have time for, as has been explained in Chapter 12. This time however, add another purpose — to attract the notice of eligible good men.

Second, once you are in the company of men, you may be faced with another problem. You may have to attract his attention away from thousand-and-one other things he may be absorbed in. He may be interested in other attractive girls, or deeply engrossed in conversation with men, or may have a problem on his mind, or be lost in thoughts about his future.

If you are to gain his notice, you will have to use the method of the salesman and distract his attention away from these things.

How to Attract His Attention

The method you will use to win the attention of men is as follows: Display any of the qualities of Angela Human, but particularly rely upon these three:

1. Appearance

2. Feminine or girlish manner

3. Feminine need or "beauty in distress"

These will be your leaning posts in attracting the notice of men. Let's give these three methods our attention.

1. The Appearance that Fascinates. Appearance is one of the keys in getting men to notice you. Turning again to the businessman, he says that "even when I have an article of great worth, I cannot afford to sit back and wait for people to come and ask for it. A great deal of study must be put upon the appearance of the product, the way in which it is wrapped or packed, so that the appearance alone will suggest its merit.

For example, I sell, among other things, a high-grade perfume. If I packed that perfume in a soda bottle and a cheap carton, it might be the finest perfume on earth, but people would not believe it worth having. I therefore pack that perfume in an exquisitely shaped and tinted cut glass bottle, with a satin lined case. This suggests the dainty exquisiteness of the perfume itself."

The same is true with a worthy girl. Her worth must be self-evident. Just as the exquisite perfume must be exquisitely presented, so must the angelic, adorable, tender and gentle girl present herself in an appearance worthy of her true character.

A woman of great worth must not be concealed under unfeminine clothes or disguised by a slouchy appearance. To do so would be like putting the expensive perfume in a soda pop bottle.

We have already studied the appearance that men notice. Clothes that are fascinating to men are feminine or girlish, in sharp contrast with the clothes that men wear. We have also learned of the astonishing effect such an appearance has on men.

If you will remember, back in the chapter on femininity I told the incident of the young woman who walked down the street in a sharply tailored brown outfit and did not receive even so much as a single admiring glance. When the same girl dressed in a feminine blue outfit, every man she passed noticed her.

I also told of the girl who went to the market time after time in an ordinary dress, and not a single man noticed her. When she went in the long, vivid flowing purple dress, three employees asked her if she would like a job working there.

Men cannot resist us when we look ravishingly feminine, but when dressed in drab masculine clothing we simply do not have much appeal.

The Sunday Child

You may have noticed this same contrast in the clothing of little children. For example, the appeal that a little girl of four makes in a plain soiled dress, ragged stockings, and untidy hair is quite different from the appeal which the same child makes on Sunday when dressed in lovely pink bonnet, soft organdy dress, with little pink knees dimpling above little socks and shiny slippers, and with a dainty ribbon and freshly curled hair setting off her bright little face. You might look upon the everyday child with indifference, but you cannot resist the impulse to gather up the Sunday child and press her to your heart.

Now, if this same Sunday child, instead of dressing in the lovely Sunday outfit described, should be arrayed in a sleek masculine inspired and tailored dress with severely plain dark hat, with her hair plastered down close to her head, she would hardly make any appeal whatever, especially without makeup.

If we want to attract men we will do as the salesman does and display our angelic character in an exquisite appearance that men will notice and admire. In addition to this, there are a few other points to consider.

Since each one of us is different in coloring, body structure, and type of personality, it will be wise to give careful thought to this subject and to discover the type of clothing that is most becoming to you and will enhance your own unique personality. You will need to discover your best colors, best necklines, best styles, etc.

There is much information on this subject, and we should not underestimate its value. It is a fact that what looks well on one person may look horrid on another.

Perfume can also gain positive notice of men. Since we might find it necessary to get his attention away from the many things that may be demanding his attention, perfume is a simple method that might help. If his nose is in a book he may not notice your appearance, but what he can't see he can smell. Men have always loved soft and sweet-smelling perfume, and smart women for generations have relied upon it as a method of getting men to notice them.

Most young girls of today are adept at using perfumes, but in case you are not, here are some simple rules. Wear something that suits you. You could also use pretty soaps or lotions if perfume or cologne is not easily available to you.

We have been speaking here of attracting the notice of men by means of feminine clothing and perfume but remember that there are even more important elements to charm than this.

The real charm that men find in women is a fresh glow of abundant health and radiance. This means smiles, bright eyes, rosy cheeks, etc. What nearly all men dislike is a dismal expression. A woman can be dressed in the most expensive and feminine clothes in the world, but if she also wears a deadpan or sour expression she will fail to be fascinating. The man may be momentarily attracted to her lovely clothes, but he will not be attracted to the woman wearing them.

Work on all three features of the appearance that fascinates men: femininity, fresh health and radiant happiness.

2. The Enchanting Feminine and Girlish Manner. You can also depend upon your feminine and girlish manner to attract men. When a man sees a feminine woman he is fascinated, but when he sees her in action he is also enchanted. Let us review the different traits of the feminine manner.

There are all of the motions of the body such as the walk, use of hands, facial expressions, voice, etc.

Then there are the traits of refinement, timorousness, fearfulness and submissiveness. There are also the girlish traits of teasing playfulness, sauciness; tenderness, joyfulness, and outspokenness that you can depend on to fascinate men.

Margaret, you will remember, won the attention of Gerard by first tying his ribbons in a feminine manner and then being a little self-conscious when she realized Gerard was noticing her. Dora won the attention of David by her "graceful, variable enchanting manner." The way she patted the horses, spanked her little dog, fixed the tea or shook her finger at him was appealing. She won his attention by femininity and girlishness of manner.

Becky Sharp, Amelia and Deruchette also attracted men by their manner. Becky Sharp was feminine, Amelia was tender, and Deruchette had the vivacity and teasing playfulness of a child.

In the novel Seventeen by Booth Tarkington is an illustration of how a young girl attracted the attention of a young man by her enchanting manner. The following describes the very first meeting between William Baxter, seventeen, and Miss Pratt.

Miss Pratt

"He saw that she was ravishingly pretty, far prettier than any girl he knew. At least it seemed so, for it is unfortunately much easier for strangers to be beautiful. Aside from the advantages of mystery, the approaching vision was piquant and graceful enough to have reminded a much older boy of the spotless white kitten, for in spite of a charmingly managed demureness there was precisely that kind of playfulness somewhere expressed about her.

"When he saw how pretty the girl was, his heart, his physical heart, began to do things the like of which experienced by an elderly person would have brought the doctor in haste. In addition, his complexion altered — he broke out in fiery patches. He suffered from breathlessness, from pressure in the diaphragm."

How little we know men and what goes on inside of them. We probably have only a slight comprehension of the way in which a fascinating woman can turn a man's heart upside down. If we knew, we would exercise our feminine charms oftener.

Using Your Eyes

One part of the feminine manner that you can always depend upon to win the notice of men is your eyes. This does not mean an old-fashioned fluttering of the eyes and a blush behind a fan, as was considered charming in colonial days. Nor does it mean a sexy "coy" glance. The charming manner of using the eyes is an almost seeming shyness, as was described in the chapter on femininity.

The method is this: When you see a man whom you want to notice you, try to get his attention by looking at him. As soon as he looks at you, when you catch his glance, look directly into his eyes for a just a moment. After a second, lower your eyes or look to the side. A longer look is far too aggressive and can even be vulgar, but a brief glance is feminine. Women have also used this skill for generations.

3. Winning Attention by Feminine Reliance. The most effective way of winning the attention of men is by feminine reliance or need for masculine care.

There is nothing that will cause a man to notice a woman sooner than her need of his assistance. You may remember that an old fashioned feminine ploy of women a few generations ago was to drop their handkerchief in hopes that men would notice them. In that period of time, women wore corsets, and it was very difficult for them to bend over to pick up anything. Men, realizing their plight, quickly came to their assistance.

There are many situations in which a woman can call on a man for help and in so doing gain his attention. By inviting situations that require the assistance and protection of men, you have an opportunity for them to begin to notice you. Your apparent need of help has made them feel masculine. Men cannot help but notice women who cause them to feel manly.

We have now covered the three most reliable methods of attracting the attention of men — by a fascinating appearance, an enchanting manner, and by feminine dependency or need.

We will now turn our attention to some practical applications. These next four examples are from the early 1900's but are still charming and can be adapted for today.

Miss Charming

Miss Charming never stays home longer than absolutely necessary. She is always gadding about where she can be seen and noticed. Wherever a group of men can be found and the presence of girls can in any way be sanctioned, there will you find Miss Charming with all her charms. Not only does she advertise herself by being everywhere, but she also takes pains to appear at her best. Her hair is always arranged in just the fashion most becoming to her, her face is made up with just the right amount of cosmetics, and her dress, which she has often made herself, is always the most girlish and feminine to be found. Her shoes and hose are neat and trim and her skirt just the right length. She sees to it, whether consciously or unconsciously, that in any crowd of girls she stands out as one of the most feminine.

While other girls are discussing sports or personalities, she is making a last-minute check on her appearance, fixing a stray hair, eyeing herself in the mirror. She is never unconscious that she is a woman and that men are around who might notice her. She is ever on the alert for their appreciative glances. A man might gaze a minute or two at another girl, deliberately weigh her charms, and decide whether or not he is interested, all without detection; but he cannot this calmly decide matters for himself with Miss Charming. Let him but steal a glance in her direction and he is immediately detected.

She lets him catch her eye, then, after looking directly into his eyes for a brief moment, drops her eyes to the floor in pretty confusion. Can anything be better calculated to attract a man's attention? In winning the attention of men, take care that you do not appear as an aggressive girl. This will put off many men. Your approach must be subtle — never aggressive.

A Stroll Through the Park

Imagine that you and a girlfriend take a stroll through the park and meet two young men, one who is known to your girlfriend and the other who is introduced. If you are dressed in feminine attire you may already have won their notice, and for want of something better to do they accompany you for a time. What can you do to attract their attention?

The first thing to do is to get to where there is some opportunity for you to need their manly assistance. Begin adventuring in the rougher parts of the park, crossing brooks, stepping stones, climbing in and out of gullies, etc. You can find many occasions where it will be harder to help yourself and where the young men can have the pleasure of demonstrating their superior agility and strength.

Every time one of them takes your hand to help you over this or that obstacle, he feels the contrast between your womanliness and his manhood. This is a good feeling for him to have and a feeling that is a genuine pleasure for him.

By the time the afternoon has passed, he will be impressed with the fact that you are an exceptionally womanly little creature and that, incidentally, he is a genuine man himself.

Very likely he will ask for the opportunity to take you to the park or the woods again, if only for the sake of again experiencing that pleasurable sensation of strength and ability.

Making the Most of a Picnic

If you are on a picnic, follow a similar feminine strategy as for the park. Don't sit down and expect to gain any masculine attention by mere gossip. Don't stay in one spot and give the men no chance to help you.

Allow yourself to get into one predicament after another where you can reasonably expect a man to offer his help. Giving his manly aid and guidance is something he very much enjoys in his association with women.

Collect a group to go adventuring, and then use every opportunity to let the men show their superior strength and agility and daring, and above all their ability to make light of the things that might intimidate you. Many a girl has attracted a man's attention to her femininity by being afraid of a mouse, snake or spider, a storm or a rickety bridge where she can reasonably cling to a man for more security. If none of these things intimidate you, find some that do.

The Railroad Trestle

There once was a girl so frightened when crossing a railroad trestle with a man, so afraid of falling through, that the man offered to carry her over. The modest little thing naturally became even more frightened at such a proposal; she blushed, became confused, and finally became so daintily reproachful that the man was enchanted. And when he finally persuaded her to place her confiding, trusting hand in his and throw herself upon his manly guidance, she maintained such an air of modest hesitancy, and yet faith in his superior strength and courage, that he could never forget the occasion.

The contrast between this timid creature and his own confident, danger scorning self-made him feel twice the man he was before.

When Being Teased

Men are usually fond of teasing women. This situation affords a wonderful opportunity to attract attention by displaying a feminine manner. The girl who can't be teased and responds only with indifference, insult or boredom, or by turning the tables on the men themselves, is missing her best chance. That sort of conduct does not make the man feel masculine, stronger or bolder.

The girl who inspires this feeling is not fascinating to a man, no matter how attractive she may be in appearance.

The genuinely feminine girl will appear to be utterly dismayed by the teasing, will bite her lip in helplessness or rage and stamp her foot in frustration until the man takes pity on her. It is a case of "beauty in distress."

A good man will naturally try to help her, to comfort her, to repair the injury to her feelings. Everything he does brings home to him the contrast between this tender, sensitive creature and his own rude, rough and masculine self.

Winning Notice at a Fair or Public Gathering

If you happen to meet a man at a fair or other crowded place, you can suggest to him by a word or glance that you would be interested in viewing some of the displays or exhibitions, but crowds around you make it somewhat impossible. You are a "beauty in distress" again and the man will most likely display his manhood by offering to guide you. After he has done so, and after your charming eyes have indicated that you admire this big strong man who has been able to do for you something you could not do for yourself, your acquaintance begins to feel a sense of importance so enjoyable that he is likely to keep steering you around for the entire afternoon and ask to assist you on some other occasion. Thus, his attention is secured.

The attractive girl makes a constant appeal for assistance, for guidance and for protection. Her eyes are always appealing to some man or another to help her in her difficulties. She never bluntly asks for help. Manly men never scorn feminine women and their need for masculine help. It contrasts his strength which compliments and pleases him.

A crowded street corner or intersection is another place a woman can be in need of masculine assistance and thus succeed in gaining a man's notice of her. Her timidity and confusion at the sight of the heavy traffic might bring nearby chivalrous gentlemen to her rescue.

How Character Can Win Attention

Although we rely upon a fascinating appearance, enchanting manner and need of masculine help to make men notice us, any of the traits of Angela Human can attract a man's attention.

It is possible that the very first thing he will notice, after your feminine appearance and manner, is a display of character on your part.

Men are looking too for companions too and good men usually are wise enough to want a girl of worth. They may not be consciously on the alert to notice character, but they certainly unconsciously will. They may be impressed by some noble deed, some kindness to child or an animal, or respect and obedience to parents.

Attracting a Man's Attention Through Your Domestic Side

Most men love it when a girl can cook and even sew, who loves little children and knows how to keep a house neat and clean. Although he may only have these skills in the back of his mind, any display of these feminine arts may quickly gain his attention.

The first time David Copperfield met Agnes, one of the first things he noticed was that "she was a staid and discreet little housekeeper."

One man told me that he was first attracted to his wife when she was sitting in a circle of girls and he happened to peek in her sewing basket and found that there were many different colors of embroidery thread, all neatly arranged. He was a man who particularly appreciated tidiness. This was quite different from the sewing baskets of his sisters, whom he had always considered quite disorderly. Though this was a small trait, it was an indication to him of greater abilities. He married the girl and found out that his judgment was correct.

Another man was invited to a dinner party in which several girls prepared the meal. The young women had drawn slips for the part of the meal they were to prepare. The vegetable was considered the least opportunity to show any special domestic skill to the men, but the girl who drew this part took it to heart and did such a marvelous job of cooking broccoli with cheese sauce that all of the men present commented only upon that part of the meal. Men will especially be apt to notice the ability to cook, and fortunately it is here that we have the greatest opportunity to show our domestic skill.

We have learned that in order to be attractive to men we must first have a fascinating appearance, which includes feminine clothes, radiant happiness and health. We add to this a feminine and girlish manner in our walk, voice, hands, etc., and also the charming feminine traits of daintiness and refinement, and feminine traits of sauciness, teasing playfulness, tenderness of emotion, joy and outspokenness.

To further gain the attention of men we can display our feminine need for masculine assistance. By naturally being a "beauty in distress," we give men the wonderful experience of playing the part of the man and hero. If you review the different traits that attract men, you will see that they all fall on the human side. Femininity, radiance, health and childlikeness (girlishness) are all human characteristics. Although we can win a man's attention in any of the qualities of Angela Human, the traits that we rely upon are the human characteristics. They are fascinating.

Chapter 22

Winning a Man's Interest

We now come to the third part of our plan for attracting men. We were told by the salesman that he could not depend upon his exquisite perfume, exquisitely presented, to sell itself, but that he had to resort to every art known to advertising and salesmanship to create an interest in it.

Similarly, a young lady, although she is a highly desirable girl, and although she has the appearance and the manner of such a girl, cannot depend upon these factors alone. There may be many other girls with similar qualifications. In order to cause the man to fall in love with her, she will have to exercise all the feminine skill and diplomacy at her command. Our next step, then, is to arouse his interest.

Method of Arousing Interest

In arousing interest, you can rely upon two basic steps to guide you. They are:

1. Inspire him to confide.

2. Admire the masculine in him.

A man's most central need, as you will remember, is to be admired for his masculine traits — his strength, aggressiveness, idealism, manly courage and determination; his proficiency in his field of study or work; and his masculine skills and abilities.

Admiring him fully for every manly trait that is within him will awaken his interest more than any other method. This task is easy. If you can get him to confide, to tell you things in which these traits are a factor, then expressing admiration will be natural and easy. And if you can get him to open his heart to you, he may reveal a whole store of things about himself in a very short time.

There are sometimes that admiration is even easier. If a man has just received an honor, or won a game, or demonstrated some skill, then a compliment for his work is effortless. But these occasions may not be plentiful enough for a girl who is trying to awaken romantic interest.

She must seek the more frequent traits of manhood to admire and then find a subtle means of expressing it. The two reasons, then, for getting a man to confide are:

1. Finding enough things to admire

2. Finding a suitable means of expressing admiration — a means that is natural, subtle and spontaneous.

How to Encourage a Man to Confide

Unfortunately, the task of getting a man to confide is easy if you understand men. Men tend to go into a shell, or his wall of reserve, as we read about in Chapter Six. Although he longs to confide in someone, so that he can be admired, he seldom does because of this wall of reserve. This reserve is caused by fear — the fear that his innermost thoughts will not be appreciated, or that they may even be treated with indifference or ridicule. The man's big problem, then, is two conflicting feelings. The first is his desire to be validated, and the second is his tendency to protect himself.

To get a man to confide, you must gain his trust, so his reserve will disappear. Now, this is not an easy task for most girls, but it can be done by following certain definite steps.

The first thing to do is to find out what his interests are. You may have observed some of them yourself, or you may have heard about them in conversations with others. If not, you will have to make a shrewd guess. Remember that men will be interested in things that concern men. They will be interested in sports, their studies, their work, special talents, skills, hobbies, world affairs, social conditions, religion, money, success, creative ideas, etc. Of all of these things, the man will only be interested in those things he is involved in or excels in.

For example, he is interested in sports because he can display a certain skill and knowledge in them; he is interested in politics or religion because he has a few pet ideas on the subject. He is interested in certain fields of study because he feels he has talents or knowledge in those areas. His interests in matters are in the way that he relates to them or contributes to them. Try to make a shrewd guess as to just what his interests might be by engaging in conversation.

The next thing to do is to subtly make a suggestion or two about this interest or indicate that you know something about what he is doing, or that you suspect him of having some big or daring venture up his sleeve. Most men will begin talking with such an invitation. Of course, his reserve will not permit him to confide in you immediately his innermost hopes and ambitions, but he will, in most cases, say enough to see if there is any remote possibility of appreciation on your part. Look for a way to appreciate him.

No matter what he says, you must look for something which you can admire. If he speaks of details of his hobby or school —things that are of little interest to you, don't betray any indifference. He will otherwise assume that your indifference is to him personally, and not to what he says. If you are successful in winning his confidence on small matters, he may venture to confide some of the more important things.

Do not be satisfied with this, however. Remember, he must trust you if you are to win his confidence and thus his romantic interest in you. Men long for admiration, but this instinctive desire is curbed in a sensitive and masculine man by his horror of making a fool of himself. That is why he will often hesitate a long time before indulging this desire. It is why he will first endeavor to find out whether his precious thoughts will be appreciatively received. He will tend to cautiously experiment with less important confidences in order to determine, by the reception of these, whether he is safe in going further.

You can now encourage further confidences. He can be brought to feel that when it comes to you, he need not withhold his confidences. He will realize he can confide his motives and aspirations to you without the least fear of ridicule or disrespect. You will interpret them in the most favorable way and will appreciate his character all the more because of the confidence he has placed in you.

Gratified by this appreciation, he will try other confidences. As these are met with encouragement, he will finally lay his heart bare before you that you may know what a wonderful man he is. You will then admire in him the sincerity, strength and determination of his manly character.

If you find it difficult to get a man to say anything at all about himself, take steps to win his confidence and break down his reserve in other ways. Go back and read the section about reserve in Chapter Three and concentrate on the steps to "breaking down his wall of reserve." Let him know that you have a sympathetic and appreciative character that always sees the best in everyone you meet. You could do this by finding something appreciative to say about everyone you know and finding the good things to admire in everyone's character. Never belittle, critical or fault finding.

Choose a person to talk about who has just been the subject of some unfair criticism. Deliberately defend the person and show what a sympathetic and trusting person you really are. This will help to reduce his fear that his ideas may be met with indifference or ridicule. You can also talk about experiences you have had, or ideas which demonstrate your understanding character.

If you are not in reality an angelic person, if you have a tendency to be critical or belittling, with an eye open for the faults in everyone, it will be difficult to disguise your underlying attitude. And even if you are clever enough to deceive the man into marrying you under false pretenses, you will never hold his love and devotion unless you are the kind of woman he thinks you are. You don't have to be perfect. He isn't either. You need to show sincere interest and appreciation for him however.

The method suggested here is not one of technique alone. You are selling yourself as a girl worth having; indicating to the man that you have qualities of sympathy and love which he has never realized you had until now.

Getting the man to talk about himself does not mean that you be too inquisitive, ask too many questions, or urge him to tell you things he is uncomfortable with. Nor does it mean that your interest be too obvious. The task is best accomplished by being subtle and by asking leading questions or making supportive comments.

When you have altogether overcome the man's reserve, he will reveal his masculine side. When you have offered to him a sincere admiration for these traits, you have awakened in him the wonderful feeling of manliness. It is at this point that you arouse his romantic interest. Strange as it may seem, when a man is interested in a certain girl, he is also interested in the pleasure, the comfort and the feeling of strength and manliness that her society gives him. This is a great method of arousing interest.

Of course, femininity and girlishness can also arouse interest, as well as angelic character and domestic traits, for they all make a man feel masculine. But in the different stages of attracting men, certain things are found to be more effective in a particular stage than others. Admiration is the one that is the most intensely effective in arousing positive attention.

While you are endeavoring to arouse interest, you will have to make certain that you do not indulge in some common mistakes that drive men away. The following suggestions are given to alert you to these mistakes.

Mistakes that Drive Men Away

If you are trying to attract a man who, you aren't sure is interested in you, follow these guidelines. If he is already in love with you, you may not have to pay as close attention to some of these suggestions, such as concealing your feelings from him. Men love to know they are loved back. But still, take care not to move faster than he does.

1. Husband Hunting. In showing a friendly interest in a man and admiring the manly things he says and does, care must be taken that you do not appear to be "husband hunting." There is nothing that will frighten a man away more quickly than to suspect that a girl is going after him. Thus, in winning a man's confidence, you must indicate by your manner that your interest is primarily the interest you would have in anyone who is a real man and does manly things. You might even intimate how you admire certain other men for this or that quality — not in a way that would discourage his hope of winning admiration from you. If this is cleverly done he may feel

challenged to tell you a few things about himself to prove to you that he is as worthy of admiration as others are. When he wins your increased admiration as a result of his own efforts, he will not suspect you of an ulterior motive.

Often when men are interested in and enjoy the society of certain girls, they are driven away by their manifest inclination to take things seriously. Remember, then, that even though a man may show a genuine interest in you, he may want to go no further than the enjoyment of your friendship. He wants to be friends with you and likes to imagine that you want merely to be friends with him. You meet each other, in his opinion, merely as an enjoyable pastime. Men want to have a companionship of this nature with a few attractive girls, but seldom anything more. Keep your relationship on this basis and you will not frighten him away.

Most men are anxious to continue a friendship with girls who do not spoil the fun by taking matters too seriously. Such girls are hard to find. Get the man to think that he is "safe" with you, that there is no danger of anything serious, and he will not hesitate to associate with you frequently. A mere suggestion on your part that you are taking things too seriously, even when he delights in your company, can cause him to shun you altogether. Remember the nature of man. He was born with the instinct to pursue the woman — the woman to be pursued. When someone tries to take away this natural situation it is confusing to the man and will likely frighten him away.

2. If You Major in Home Economics. Letting a man know that your field of study is home economics, child development, marriage, family relations, may give him the impression that

you are husband hunting. There are so many girls who are too forward with men — who do not know how to be subtle in their approach — that men are inclined to be "on guard" for these girls and are alert to little evidences of this aggressive attitude.

It will therefore be wise to not deliberately indicate to a man that this is your educational interest. Men, of course, want women to be domestic, and notice little evidences of skill like cooking and sewing, but these seem less "husband hunting" if they appear to be skills learned at home.

If the man asks directly about your course of study, answer honestly, but with the attitude that "this is what every young woman should take, regardless of her plans for the future." Whatever you do, don't give him the impression that you are overly anxious to get married.

3. Conceal Your Feelings from Him. As you are trying to awaken a man's interest, if you find that you are falling in love with him, you will have to take care that you do not let these feelings show. A safe rule is this: Never give an indication that you like him more than he likes you. Let the man lead in feeling and you follow. There is a time that he will welcome you telling him you love him, but this will be only after he is genuinely interested in you.

Hiding feelings is extremely difficult to do and there are few girls who master it. A young girl especially tends to make mistakes. The exuberant tone in her voice when he calls on the phone, the light in her eyes when he arrives, the way she looks at him in contrast to all the other men are all dead "giveaways."

Though men are flattered at a woman's interest, if she moves too fast it might put him off.

Any girl, for that matter, finds it a challenge to conceal her feelings from a man she is in love with until he has a chance to be in love with her. One girl told me an interesting solution. When her boyfriend was to arrive she became so excited and glowing that she was certain he would be able to detect her feelings. To solve this problem, she went into the bedroom and pounded her fists on the wall to let some of it out. Then she was able to act casual when he arrived.

4. Hide Your Feelings From Others. If you are seriously interested in a man, do not make the mistake of revealing this fact to anyone, not even your best friend. Girls cannot always be trusted with this information, and even though they may not be so foolish as to tell the man himself, they may tell other girls or even other boys. News such as this travels quickly.

Boys in dorms sometimes engage in gossip sessions, and often the subject for discussion is women. Do not rely upon extracting promises from girls either. There have been too many promises broken, too many secrets revealed, and too many men frightened away by such a disclosure.

If you could be certain that the man's feelings for you were as deep as your own, or more so, then he would delight in knowing the facts, but unless you are certain, play it safe and keep your feelings to yourself. Trust no one with the exception of possibly your parents.

5. Falling Off Your Pedestal. Another thing which can cause a good man to lose interest in you is for you to fall off your

pedestal by showing some weakness in character. By lowering your standards, by making some harsh or critical remark, or by a lazy or slovenly attitude in your work, his interest in you could weaken. He may feel that you are much less of a woman than he had thought.

How to Keep Him Guessing

There is nothing that will sustain a man's interest in you more than "keeping him guessing." This, again, is for the period of time before you are certain he is in love with you. This means, do not give him the satisfaction of knowing just how you feel about him.

A woman is more intriguing to a man if he isn't sure where he stands with her. The way to do it is this:

Be friendly with him — but also be friendly with everyone else. In this way he will never quite detect whether your friendliness with him is just your nature or whether you are in love with him. If you are somber around most people and then light up when he walks by you will be "wearing your heart on your sleeve." It will be obvious how you feel. If, on the other hand, you light up around everyone, he never quite knows.

Then, don't be too available. Date him, but also date other men. If he has been seeing too much of you recently, when he calls "arrange to be busy." If you don't have a date with someone else, then you have "too much homework," or "unexpected home duties," or "have promised to spend the night with a girlfriend." Caution should be taken here however. If he is already in love with you and you do some of these things, he might get discouraged and give up on you, mistakenly thinking you do not share his feelings. But in the early stages of a relationship where you are still trying to win his love, this advice comes in very handy.

One good way to keep a boy guessing is to have an absorbing interest in life, and particularly your own activities or responsibilities. If you work, let him know that you are interested in it and enjoy it. Show an interest in special hobbies, talents and other activities, and devote a certain amount of your time and energy to them. This will relieve him of any feeling that you may be hunting for a husband.

Intensifying Interests

When you have aroused a man's interest in you by winning his confidence and admiring the manly, you have made considerable progress. If you continue this treatment, you will intensify his interest by one of the most powerful influences known to bring a man and woman together, fascination of secrets you have shared with each other.

You know things about him and his aspirations that are known to no one else; you have been trusted with confidences that have not been exposed to the criticism and appreciation of another. Nor must it be forgotten that you feel a difference between him and other men. You have given confidences as well as received them. This man knows about your ideals and your aspirations and difficulties. He understands and appreciates and reverences you as men who know less about you could never do. You and he are in a class by yourselves, apart from all the rest of the world in each other's estimation.

When you meet your eyes flash in understanding and sympathy when others are absorbed in other matters. You encourage one another by word and look. Whether at church, a party, in the classroom or at a sporting event you cannot help singling each other out as being different and on a different footing from all mankind. You have secrets between you that others do not and cannot share. His interest then is intensified, which will provide a transition from interest to romantic love.

Let me remind you again of the utmost necessity of keeping your secrets confidential. And be sure that there is no relationship between you that is unwholesome or shameful in any way. Continue to win his confidence and offer him admiration, and thus sustain the interest until it grows into love.

Creating a Desire

Going back to the salesman again and his method of helping to create a desire, what does he do? He goes from approach that he used in winning attention and creating interest and begins to sell his customer on the quality of the product itself and how indispensable it is to their welfare and happiness.

He must do this before he can bring them to any kind of decision to buy the product — before he can create in them a desire for it. You can use this same approach in helping the man you love to return your affections. You will not depend upon strategy and tactics. It will not be a result of what you do, but what you are.

You will have to prove that you are a girl worth having and that you are indispensable to his happiness. These are the two steps that you can use in creating this desire:

1. Prove you are a girl worth having.

2. Become indispensable to his happiness.

To prove your worth, you will have to take work on having the qualities of Angela Human. I encourage you to review all of those chapters and get well in your mind all of the component parts that make up the ideal woman, and then work with all diligence to be like her. Work on character, the domestic skills, and inner happiness and all of understanding men.

Concentrate again on femininity and childlikeness, as well as radiant happiness and health. This may seem like quite an undertaking, but it is surprising what a girl can do when she realizes her future happiness is at stake and that attracting the man she loves depends so much upon her.

Seek the Lord in prayer and ask Him to help you become the tender, angelic and fascinating woman that He designed you to be. If you have a picture in your mind of the girl you ought to be, and ask for God's help, it will be surprising what He can do. Your understanding of the subject will broaden, and your ability to be the ideal woman will seem more like second nature to you. And once you come close enough to this ideal to win the man you adore, if you want to hold his love for a lifetime you will have to continue to be Angela Human and strive every day to be the kind of woman a man wants. When the Lord knows of your high and noble goals, not only of winning the man you love but of keeping him happy for a lifetime, He will not turn you away if the man is right for you.

Keep this image of Angela Human firmly in your mind then, and constantly strive to be like her. Work with all energy of both mind and heart.

Become Indispensable to Him

To be indispensable means that you have something the other person cannot get along without.

Because of this he has grown to believe you are essential to his well-being and happiness.

To be essential to a man we reach one of his most vulnerable parts, his great need for understanding. By supplying him with all of the different elements of true understanding, by giving him admiration, sympathy and comfort in times of need, and by sharing with him his joys and sorrows, a woman can without a doubt be indispensable to a man.

Up to now, a man may have been pretty independent, at least since he reached manhood. He has found his own comforts, healed his own wounds and supplied his own emotional needs. He may have relied upon close friends and parents, but no one person has become, to him, indispensable to his welfare and happiness. But you can change all of this and make him connected to you so that he will rely upon you for comfort in difficulty, for sympathy and true understanding. We are need men for protection and masculine care, but they can become reliant upon us for a different kind of need. One that only a feminine woman can give.

The way to become indispensable is this: First, continue to admire his masculinity, since this will intensify interest until it automatically grows to the point of romantic love. He will begin to feel that you are essential to him because you are the only woman who can make him feel really manly. This in itself is an indispensable feeling for a man. But even more important, you will find that if you continue to admire the manly you will further win his confidence so that he will turn more and more to you. Then you will have the opportunity to supply his other emotional needs that only a feminine woman can do.

When he has some new idea or plan, he will long to discuss it with someone, but he dares not discuss it with anyone but you, for you are the only woman who could possibly understand and appreciate his ideas.

When he meets with a rebuff or criticism from others, the most natural thing for him to do is to turn to you. When the feeling comes to him, as it comes at times to every man, that he is not the man he ought to be, that he has not lived up to the best that is in him, the only person he knows who can make him feel like a worthwhile masculine man again is you.

When his plans meet with discouragement he knows that he will find solace and understanding in your presence. Or, when his plans meet with glorious success, his fondest hopes seem about to be realized, where should he turn but to you, the only one who he truly trusts to share his joy and happiness with complete understanding.

As this feeling intensifies, he finds it more and more difficult to live without you, more and more necessary to have you with him as the life-long sharer of his joys and sorrows. This is a considerable removal from the apathy with which he began. The difference in his eyes between you and all other women assumes prodigious proportions. You have become indispensable to his well-being and happiness. You did not seem indispensable before, but that was just because he did not know what real joy and happiness were until you inspired him with these feelings.

If you have also proven you are a girl worth having, he has suddenly begun to realize that you are everything he has ever wanted in a woman — an inspiring character and yet a human bundle of girlish femininity. At this point you begin to inspire love for you in the man, a desire to have you for his own.

Along with desire, you awaken another feeling in his heart —his love. By becoming Angela Human you have inspired the feelings of worship, adoration, the tender desire to protect and shelter you. You have caused him to be fascinated, amused and enchanted, and have awakened all of the thrilling and consuming sensations of romantic love. These feelings combine to form the many-splendored feeling called love.

Is anything better that can help bring a man to the point of this kind of desire? It is the combination of these overwhelming feelings that can cause a man to make the jump to marriage, that can cause him to sacrifice his freedom, tax his usually limited resources, undertake the heavy responsibilities of marriage and attempt the often-difficult task of being the main bread winner for the girl he loves.

Maintaining Interest While You Inspire Love

Love is sometimes slow to grow, so don't become impatient with this step of gaining his love. You can sustain his interest while love Has time to grow into deeper awareness. Though we cannot rely upon psychology to turn interest to desire, we can rely upon it to maintain interest until desire has grown. All you need to do is to use the principles of arousing interest while romantic love develops.

This means that you continue to win his confidence, that you continue to admire the manly in him, and along with this use every opportunity to give him the understanding and sympathy that every man needs.

The disadvantage of many girls is that they do not maintain interest long enough to give the man's attraction time to grow. You are under no such disadvantage; you can maintain his interest as long as is required to give his emotions time to develop into real love. You only need a little time to let nature arouse in the man the desire to have you for himself.

And while you are working on maintaining interest, you can work on all of the qualities of Angela Human. During this time, it is essential that you do not undo the progress you have made by making mistakes that could spoil the whole thing. During the time of inspiring love, take care that you do not make the following mistakes:

Don't be Too Obvious

Don't make the mistake of showing your feelings until you are certain his feelings are reciprocated. And don't tell him that you love him until he has said he loves you. It puts him in an extremely awkward situation.

Don't move faster than he does. The man most often enjoys being the pursuer, the girl the pursued. If you tell him you love him before he has made up his mind about you, you might stop his pursuit. It depends on the man and his personal confidence level. Be wise. Some men need a little encouragement, but it can be taken too far.

Don't be Aggressive

Don't be physically aggressive, since this deprives a man of his masculinity. Don't squeeze close when he is driving; don't put your lips up to be kissed or reach for his hand during a movie, etc. This can kill a romance if done too early. Don't send him notes unless they are answers to his. You need to encourage masculinity and reward his growing confidence in his relationship with you.

Don't Fall from Your Pedestal

When a man is trying to decide about you is the time he might shake your pedestal or test your character to see if you are the angelic creature you appear to be. He may try to see what your limits are and how far you'll go if pushed even a little. If he respects you, he will appreciate you holding firm to your convictions. If he rejects you for not complying with his desires, he would have anyway and was just using you. Don't disappoint him by lowering your standards, making a sharp critical remark, or doing some unkind or selfish deed, or showing some other weakness of character.

Premature Physical Affection

During this time that love is growing is when a girl and a boy are most apt to be affectionate. Unless you are certain that he is in love with you, and you with him, it is dangerous to engage in too much physical affection for the following reasons:

1. It will bring into play emotions that will make it difficult for true love to develop, and it may confuse both of you. Even if you are certain that you love him, it may cloud the issue for him. His feelings and interest in you may be only physical. How can he really tell how he feels about you? The emotions of sexual attraction are meant to accompany love and not to precede it.

2. You cheapen yourself when you can be had without love. Also, he will think, "If you give me affection so easily, do you also give it to other men casually?" By safeguarding too much physical affection until you are certain you have his love, you put a special value on it.

3. It stirs the emotions to greater passions such as sex, which leads us to the next problem to consider.

Don't Indulge in Sex Before Marriage

When a relationship grows from affection into a sexual experience the problems are multiplied many times. Most girls do not realize the dangers involved for them emotionally, physically and every other way.

Not only is it morally wrong to have sex before marriage, but it is very foolish. Consider the following thoughts on this subject:

1. When a woman becomes involved with a man sexually, she almost always becomes involved with him emotionally as well. Ending the affair can be a crushing blow to her. This is not apt

to be so as often with the man. Surveys show that eighty percent of the men who engage in premarital sex do not necessarily even like the girl. Having no emotional attachment, they are apt to "love her and leave her," free of any obligation of marriage.

2. Marriage is a protection to a woman. Marriage says, "Give me first your name, and promise to be mine, and then I will trust you enough to let you to engage in sex with me." The girl who yields before marriage removes this protection as a woman.

3. Giving sex without marriage cheapens a girl in the man's eyes. Men insist upon placing a value on everything, including their women. If they can have you for nothing, they don't value you as much.

4. Some girls yield because they are afraid of losing the man if they say no. Actually, just the opposite is true. If she surrenders, she may win him as a bed partner, but is less likely to win him in marriage. Surveys show that only ten percent of men who engage in premarital sex marry the girl involved.

In returning to the subject of creating desire and winning the man's love, you will need to avoid these mistakes. Don't let your feelings show too early, control physical affection until love grows and don't yield in sex lest you undermine your relationship and reap only heartache and disappointment.

Instead, concentrate on awakening real love in his heart by acquiring the qualities of Angela Human, by being a girl worth having. As you continue to give him admiration, sympathy, comfort and hope, sharing his every joy and sorrow, you will find you are indispensable to his true happiness. He will begin to feel that he cannot live without you.

Because of your feminine nature, he will begin to think of himself as the only one who can appreciate your womanliness, the only one who can properly protect you and provide for you as you deserve. He feels that it is imperative for him to look after you — that you are his to watch and shield and provide for. His attention has grown into interest, his interest has grown into worship, and his worship is now full-fledged love.

In reviewing the method of creating desire, we have found that it is accomplished in two steps. The first is to prove you are a girl worth having, and the second is to make yourself indispensable to the man's happiness. Both of these goals are reached by becoming Angela Human, but the latter goal is dependent upon understanding men.

Removing the Obstacle to Marriage

If you will think back about the incident of the insurance salesman, you will remember that after he had created a desire in the mind of his customer, he then had to dispel certain doubts and fears that they might have in regard to insurance, their ability to pay the premiums, etc. — in other words, "satisfy their judgment." Only then would the customer feel confident enough to make a decision about buying insurance.

A man, too, may have certain doubts, fears and problems that present themselves as obstacles to marriage. He may wish to marry, and yet hesitate to undertake the responsibilities involved. He may have dependent relatives, or a heavy debt, or unknown obligations of many different kinds. He may be doubtful of his ability to provide for you, or too proud to ask you to share a lower standard of living than that to which you are accustomed. Or he may even be afraid that you do not return his feelings and be unwilling to risk the humiliation of a refusal.

These objections must be overcome before he will act upon his desire to marry. Not always, however, does the girl have to take the initiative to help him overcome these objections. Sometimes the man struggles with them himself, weighing out one problem against another until he overcomes these objections, without the girl doing or even knowing anything about them. But if his problems seem insurmountable, causing him to postpone the important step of marriage, the girl can sympathize with these problems and help him overcome these barriers.

Things in Your Favor

A list of the objections a man may have to marriage is enough to dishearten any girl. So valid and so obvious are they that men often don't step into matrimony deliberately. They step into it only with great emotion, when cold reason and calm judgment are out of the question.

In spite of this fact, however, you must not become discouraged. Though you should familiarize yourself with the objections he may have to marriage, and though you must recognize their importance, you must not forget that before you have reached this stage, you have already aroused in him the desire to be with you forever. He can no longer reason coldly and judge calmly; everything is colored by his desire to have you for his own. He is likely to cast discretion to the winds and, objection or no objections, ask you to be his lifetime partner.

And if he does hesitate, if he does find it impossible to overlook some of the obstacles, then he is troubled to find this objection standing between him and his desire and is just as anxious to have it removed as you are.

Overcoming objections is therefore not the tremendous task it would be if the man were not influenced by his own desires and sentiments.

The Two Barriers to Marriage

Standing between the man's desire to marry the girl and asking her consent are two classes of objections. The first class covers his objections to marrying anyone. The second class covers his objections to marrying a particular girl. We shall now consider the first class, objections to marrying anyone.

Fear that He Cannot Earn Enough Money to Support Marriage

Probably the most common cause of hesitation in a young man who likes and wants to marry a girl is that he fears he cannot earn enough or does not have enough money to support a wife. In many cases, he not only fears it, he knows it.

When this is the case, he certainly does not frankly come out and tell the girl that he would like to marry her but that he can't afford it. The girl could easily tell him, under such circumstances, what she can do to help him out or how she is willing to wait or how marriage is more economical than he anticipates. Or he may fear humiliation at this disclosure.

Instead, he might pay attention to her for months and yet give no evidence of his desire to marry. She may think he doesn't care for her at all.

As long, however, as the man continues to show interest in her, the girl should not lose heart. She should study him and try to guess what objection it is that is holding him back. If she imagines that the fear of being unable to support a wife is an obstacle, she must proceed to try to help remove it.

This is not to be done, of course, by boldly coming out into the open and showing him that he can. That would be far too aggressive and unfeminine. The following method is effective.

How to Banish His Fear of Being Able to Support a Wife

Get the man to talk about his future, his plans, his expectations and ambitions. Try to make him forget his present humble position and live in the imaginative future. Talk about his successful and glorious future as if to you it is a certain and definite thing, as if there can be no doubt about it in your mind. Before long he will begin to talk and think the same way; he will become confident in himself. His present financial circumstances will be looked upon as only temporary. Since his successful future is an agreeable subject to him it will require no great effort on your part to bring it up at every opportunity.

His superior financial status two or three years from now becomes a certainty; he looks upon himself as already made. You must together build castles in the air and it will only be a matter of two or three years before these castles will be built upon solid ground.

This attitude of mind on your part is contagious; the man too will feel that there is no doubt about what he will have to offer you two or three years hence. When a man becomes certain of his success there is no reason why he should not ask you to wait for him. And there should be no reason on your part why you should not be willing to wait.

There are often so many objections to an immediate marriage, objections which he thinks will be overcome at a later date. It therefore might be helpful for him to at least propose that you "wait for him."

Sometimes men have anxiety of setting a definite date. After the engagement is set, however, the girl can speak freely about it, and can proceed to further remove his fears and objections to marrying sooner. She can begin to point out how unnecessary it is to wait until his success has already been accomplished, how willing she is to fight through on his present salary until he can do better, how she can help to economize, and how by marriage they can save money and time and work together more efficiently than before to hasten the day when his ambition will be realized. Finally, under the spell of some moonlit night when it is difficult to say goodnight, or when he anticipates leaving town on business, etc., and it is difficult to say good-bye, they decide to marry immediately, for better or for worse, and begin their partnership in earnest. She might also agree to continue any work she has until her first baby comes along.

Fear of an Uncertain Future

Sometimes, even when a man knows he is earning enough to support a wife, he still hesitates to go ahead because he is uncertain about his future. He may be earning enough now, but is he sure that he will continue to earn enough? Maybe he will have bad luck, lose his position, or he may not feel conditions will remain the same. There is the risk that he will make less in the future than now.

There are thousands of overly cautious young men. The only thing a girl can do is to bolster his self-confidence and use the "castle in the air" psychology in much the same manner as has already been described.

This she does until he finally asks her to wait for him — to wait until he is sure that his earning ability more of a permanent thing. Once engaged he might change his mind about postponing marriage, can alter his desire to wait until things are more secure.

When a Man's Dependents Stand in the Way

Another obstacle that sometimes stands in the way of a man's ability to get married is the fact that he has a mother to support, an aged father or smaller brothers and sisters. Many men who do not appear to have dependents — especially men living alone in a big city — are obliged to send a big part of their earnings home every month to contribute to the support of others. They might have been married before and have children to support. Often, they will not divulge some such stressors because they do not like to admit that members of their families are victims of unfortunate or legal circumstances.

He may earn a comfortable salary, but because of his responsibilities he is not as free to marry as a man earning much less. At the same time, the girl may know nothing about some of this quiet claim on his support and may think he holds back because he does not desire to marry her. Because of this, a man should never be judged harshly when he hesitates, and the girl should never become impatient and give up hope.

What She Should Do

If the girl will only wait patiently, the man will sooner or later tell her about the dependents. He may not always admit that they are dependent, but he will say something from which she can surmise the facts. If they are not too far away, the girl should arrange to meet his parents and try to win their love and approval. In many cases, if she is an adorable girl, the dependents will realize that they are standing in the way of the young man's happiness and for fear that he will lose this girl whom they also love, will try to find a way by which they can ease the man's financial burdens so that he can feel free to marry. (Former spouses are an exception of course).

Whether she has the chance to meet the dependents or not, the girl should let him know that she admires his sacrifices for his family and admires him for it, that she would not under any circumstances expect him to do otherwise. The man begins to feel that if he were married to her she would not object to his using part of his income for the support of his other dependents. (She should sincerely support him on this.) Thus, part of the obstacle is removed.

To further remove his obstacles, she should follow the information outlined in the preceding problem of enthusiastically picturing his future until he feels certain that within two or three years he will make so much more money that he will be able to support a wife in spite of his other obligations. As before, all he dares do is to ask her to wait for him, but once they are engaged, she does not find it difficult to hasten things along. In the case of younger brothers and sisters being dependent upon the man, almost the only thing necessary to do, especially if they are very young, is to win their affection — an easy thing to do in the case of small children.

The obstacle would then be removed, because it would be plain to any man that he would be better able to care for children with the aid of a wife than without that aid. If the children are older, they would not be a serious obstacle, for then it would only be a matter of a few years until they are self-supporting. It should not be difficult to get the man to ask the girl to wait for that length of time.

Dependents by a Former Marriage

In the case of alimony to a former wife and children, the man is not making a noble sacrifice but is fulfilling both a moral and legal obligation. He has no choice in matters but to pay.

If he is a high-principled man and loves his children he will take it in good spirit and assume his obligation as any other.

His greatest fear may be that a new wife may not feel as he does and that he might not be able to afford an ex-wife as well as a wife. There is a tendency for some women to resent obligations accrued by a former marriage.

If you show that you accept the idea and will support him in good spirit, you will greatly relieve his fears of difficulty in marriage. Such a reassurance of your generosity and understanding will encourage his proposal in marriage.

When Debts Block the Path

Sometimes a man appears to have no obligations toward dependent relatives but has other obligations that are just as binding. For example, he may have gone into debt to finish his college education and may not have been able to pay it back yet. He may be earning only enough to support himself and have little prospect of earning more in the immediate future. Sometimes the prospects of being able to pay back these loans are slim enough without having a wife to support. This obstacle is practically impossible to overcome except by the "castle in the air" method, by reviving enthusiasm and self-assurance until he feels that his future success is so sure that he need not be afraid to ask the girl to wait for him.

Obstacles that Prevent Marriage to a Particular Girl

We now turn from the obstacles which would prevent his marriage to any girl and consider those which would prevent marriage to a particular girl. It sometimes happens that when there are no impediments to marriage in general, there is a great impediment to marriage with a particular girl.

A Man's Feelings of Inferiority

The first obstacle here, in regard to marriage with one girl in particular, is when a man may feel a distrust of himself or a sense of inferiority around a particular girl. We all know of the story of John Alden and Priscilla. John thought so much of Priscilla and so little of himself that he couldn't even hope that Priscilla would care for him. He considered Miles Standish so much better a man that the thought of rivaling him in Priscilla's affections was undreamed of. So far from proposing for himself was he, that he undertook in all seriousness to carry Miles Standish's proposal to her. Poor Priscilla finally had to ask him "Why don't you speak for yourself, John."

Now this situation is not as infrequent as one might suppose. The bravest and most self- possessed man sometimes loses his bravery and self-possession when in the presence of the girl he worships. He might feel unworthy in the presence of this angelic creature. He hesitates to put his fate to the test for fear that he will be exiled altogether. He may call on her a number of times with the intention of asking the all-important question, only to lose heart at the last moment and put it off until another time.

There is only one thing to do, and that is to take pity on him and help him along, as Priscilla did with John Alden. Many men who marry do not propose without some help from the girl. Of course, this help cannot be given except when the girl positively knows that the man wants to speak and can't. The help must be given out of pity for his misery, and not out of boldness or impatience. Unless she knows he is in misery, she should not interfere.

Too Proud to Ask

The next obstacle we shall consider is the man's pride. Perhaps he can support a wife, but only in a modest way and not at all in the way that this particular girl is accustomed. He is too proud to ask her to accept a lower standard of living just for his sake. Even when the girl comes from a modest home, pride sometimes prevents him because the man has a certain idea of the way he expects himself to maintain a household and he is too proud to risk their criticism by starting out on a more modest scale. This obstacle might be overcome the way any other economic obstacle is, by using the "castle in the air" method until he asks her to wait for him or decides to marry sooner.

When the Man's Family Objects

We now come to one of the most common obstacles of all, the objections of the man's family to a girl. It is unfortunately true in some families that a marriage of a beloved son is looked upon with the most scrutinizing eye. Even when the family does not oppose marriage in general, they may oppose his marriage to a particular girl he desires. Mothers are sometimes prone to believe that no girl is quite good enough for their sons. They will discover a thousand faults in the poor girl and will resist his desire with every resource available.

To overcome this obstacle, the girl should first endeavor to win the affection and good will of his family. In some cases, however, this is impossible. She must determine to win him without their good will.

This is not as difficult as it appears because he usually resents the unfairness of the family's attitude toward the girl and is indignant at the poor reception given the woman he loves. The active opposition of the family could, in fact, speed him to action.

If the family's opposition does not speed him to action, the girl must resort to the "castle in the air" method — to enter into his plans, hopes and ambitions so thoroughly and so sympathetically that he cannot think of his bright future without her to share it, to be an inspiration and comfort to him. He begins to feel that he cannot live without her. Then his desire will sweep aside all obstacles of whatever nature.

Summary

There are innumerable other obstacles to marriage — such as ambition, fear of the humiliation of a refusal, fear of the contempt of his social circle when he marries beneath it, the possibility of marrying a girl with wealth, doubt whether the girl's liking is permanent, etc. In any case the method for removing the obstacle is pretty much the same. Either patiently increase his desire or get him to project himself into the future and there picture success and the solution to his problems.

Chapter 25

The Proposal

In theory, all obstacles out of the way, a man proposes. It is not always as simple as this, however. The man may find that unless he has a particular reason to hurry things along, it is easier to procrastinate the important step and keep things as they are. This may go on for months, with nothing resolved and the girl wondering all the time how serious the man's feelings are for her.

If this is the case, the girl can bring him to action in any one of three general ways. The first is by making it easy for him to speak out, the second is by making it hard for him not to, and the third is by making immediate action appear urgent and necessary. The following will explain these three ways to secure action.

Method # 1: Making it Easy for Him to Act

You can make it easy for a man to act in two general ways. The first is to maintain an optimistic and enthusiastic atmosphere, as we have already explained in "creating desire" and "overcoming judgment." Continue to "build castles in the air" and this will tend to minimize the responsibilities of matrimony. In fact, this optimistic attitude of projecting a man into his bright future can in some cases carry a romance from desire, through judgment, and into action.

Not always, however, can we rely upon this approach. We sometimes have to resort to other methods. A second way of making it easy for him to act is to get him in a romantic and sentimental frame of mind.

Few men propose in a mood of cold and calculating reason. The girl should endeavor, therefore, to arouse in him the opposite of reason — a feeling of warm and deep emotion, or of dreamy, drifting surrender to sentiment. In such a mood, reason is subdued and the impulse to speak out is unopposed. The manner of awakening these sentimental moods is accomplished by creating romantic situations. A number of suggestions are given here.

Creating Romantic Situations to be Alone

The first thing to avoid is a third person. No man ever becomes truly romantic while other people are around. When more than two are present the conversation and the atmosphere becomes entirely different.

Dim Lights

The next thing to avoid is an atmosphere of bright or brilliant lights. In the glare of such lights reason is uppermost and not sentiment. The lights must be subdued to give an atmosphere of peace and comfort and to lull the nervous warnings of the man's judgment into a sentimental mood. A glow of pink thrown over everything has a "cozy" effect. In such a soft illumination a girl's hair can appear "halo like," making her appear soft and tender. They tend to converse on subjects that harmonize with the effects — tend to become confidential and dream together. Drifting thus, how easy it is for the man to gently take her hand, and in sublime forgetfulness of all of the obstacles in the outside world, whisper to her the loveliest dream of all. And how unlikely it would have been without this encouraging atmosphere.

A Cozy Winter Evening

The atmosphere can be even more suggestive of sentiment if it is winter and the wind is howling outside, and sleet is dashing against the window. How cozy and comforting it is for the girl and the boy, sitting before an open fire with the lights dimmed, to sit and dream. The man may feel that he would like for this to continue forever. There cannot be obstacles, he feels, when life is easy and peaceful as this. How easy for him to succumb to his dearest desire and forget his fears.

Spring and Summer

In the spring and summer equally, romantic effects can be secured. Sitting on a porch or patio, in a lawn swing, or any place amid the beauties of nature are romantic places. If there is a moon, so much the better. The gentle breeze stirring the leaves in the trees, the distant whistle of a train, the twilight bark of a remote but watchful dog, make the world with its problems seem far away.

Water: Lakes, Oceans and Rivers

Even in broad daylight, the effect of water is often spellbinding, especially upon those who may live daily in a crowded city. Night, water and romance are inseparable. Have you ever noticed how often people are inclined to spend their vacations or holidays on or near water? There is a reason. Nothing is more soothing, more calculated to subdue fears and draw a man and woman close to each other than a night scene on the water, with the moon and stars shining on the ripples, the gentle lap of waves upon a beach or against a boat, and the mysterious blackness of a distant shore line.

Many men have innocently taken a girl on a boating excursion at night and returned to find themselves engaged.

Parks and Gardens

A stroll through some beautiful garden, or in the hills or mountains, or in the woods, can often supply the atmosphere desired. There is nothing like getting back to nature to encourage a man to follow nature's impulse to take a mate for himself.

A Homey Atmosphere

Next to the peace and quiet of nature, the most encouraging atmosphere is the coziness and comfort of a home — an ideal home where there is a spirit of peace and an absence of quarreling, worry and tension that seem a part of the outside world.

If the girl has such an ideal home, she can use this to good advantage.

Restaurants that Encourage Romance

In many cities there seem to be two or three restaurants which seem to be especially designed to encourage romantic young couples. Such restaurants are secluded, lights are subdued, they are not crowded with too many people. If there is music, it may be quiet and romantic. With the peaceful atmosphere of such soothing surroundings and with a girl across the table whose eyes are more comforting and sympathetic even than the atmosphere, the man will be reluctant to leave and will dream of a home where every meal would be like this. It is a time for mutual confidences and sharing dreams, when you are drawn closer and closer together.

Restaurants to avoid are those that are noisy and crowded. A small one may be better than a large busy one. Avoid the dazzling white restaurants, the loud and glittering kind, and the casinos. These don't suggest coziness and contentment; their atmosphere discourages all thought of home and marriage.

A picnic lunch in the woods, in a private park or by a river can be just as comfortable and cozy as a restaurant. Give the man time enough to absorb the atmosphere and time enough to let it penetrate deeply. Never hurry through a picnic in the woods.

Movies, Plays, Concerts

If you are going to a movie and you are given the opportunity to choose, always avoid the horror type or the violent dramas. War movies are also out as far as romance is concerned, if they have an abundance of fighting and a minimum of romance in the story. These movies discourage the atmosphere you are seeking to create.

Instead choose a romantic play or dramatic story that works upon the sympathies and emotions. Try to find out in advance the value of current movies, even if you have to see them yourself before.

If, when you are leaving a romantic movie, the man has a lump in his throat, if he has a feeling that life is a lovely and beautiful thing after all, if he feels that love and character and idealism and truth are the only things that really count, then he is likely to speak out the things that weigh on his heart and forget all about money matters and other problems that have been standing in his way. The objections are not among the things that count when he is in this frame of mind. His emotions have been so wrought upon, are in such turmoil, that any impulse is without opposition. An emotional mood such as this is an impulsive mood. And if the impulse strikes him, there are not the paralyzing fears to halt it.

There are not enough such soul-stirring movies today. It may require quite a search to find an appropriate movie that stirs the emotions. If you cannot find one, it will be better to depend upon other romantic situations and skip the movies, unless of course they are his idea.

Making Plans for Yourself

Still another way to make it easy for a man to speak out is to make plans for your life which do not include marriage at the moment. Be careful with this one however. If he perceives that you do not return his great affection, he might get discouraged and not ask you. This is only a good idea if you are certain he does love you but is either taking you for granted or simply is afraid to take the plunge.

Under these circumstances, the man who has been hesitating because immediate marriage seems out of the question he will find it easy to speak out.

These are not the only methods of making it easy for a man to speak out. The girl must remember that although we can suggest general principles, each man is an individual personality requiring individual study. She must observe him carefully until she understands his character enough to make an educated guess about what makes it hard in his individual case to propose. When this has been done, she can then use her knowledge to guide her in deciding what is needed to make action easy for this particular man. She may come to the conclusion that an entirely new method, not mentioned here, should be practiced in bringing him to action.

When the man fails to respond to the first scenario of securing action, making it easy for him to speak out, he is by no means a hopeless case. She can then proceed to the second method of getting action — making it hard for him not to act.

Scenario # 2: Making it Hard NOT to Act

It should be understood throughout this chapter that there is no use trying any of the methods of stirring a man to action unless it is fairly certain that he is definitely in love with you, that he is hesitating because of inward doubts and outward obstacles.

Getting action is the last of the six steps to winning men. To attempt to make it the second, or the third, etc., is futile. If the man fails to respond to these methods, the girl can usually take it for granted that he is not ready to get married.

She must then devote her thoughts to increasing his desire or helping to get the obstacles out of the way. In securing action by making it hard not to act, the following are suggestions.

The Apology Scenario

One method is a result of the man's committing some offense towards the girl, as often happens in true romance. Sometimes a man is harsh or brutally frank, which will send the girl into a spell of gloom that can be disheartening. If she will take this occasion to let him know that he has wounded her tender feelings (after he has cooled off, of course) she will invite an apology from him. When the man is brought to an apology for having offended a tender and feminine woman, he has a tendency to condemn himself and do everything possible to relieve her feelings. In his attempt to make her feel happy again, he is very apt to also confide in her his tender feelings for her.

If a romantic setting further makes it easy for him to speak, then his thoughtlessness at having wounded her feelings will make it difficult to withhold his innermost feeling of love and tenderness for her. In other words, it makes it hard for him not to speak out, or to act. He must be encouraged into a position where he feels like a "brute" and must make amends, that an ordinary apology will appear to be inadequate, and that an elaborate expansion of his feelings towards the girl is required.

If the man is in love with the girl, and if the obstacles have been temporarily minimized, such an apology often leads into a declaration of love and a proposal.

The Rescue Scenario

Another method of making it hard not to act, is the "rescue "method or the "beauty in distress" method. This is the story line used by so many novelists. The heroine is the center of some misfortune and trouble and the man is inspired to come to her rescue. This situation, however, is not nearly so frequent in real life as it is in fiction.

The nearest the average girl can come to it is by the method of being sad and disconsolate because of problems in the future which seem to her unsolvable. In some circumstances, however, misfortune and trouble do come, such as the girl being pressed to marry someone she dislikes, or her family meets with financial disaster, or the girl loses her position or sees someone get the promotion on which she had depended, etc.

In these cases, if the girl will tactfully let the man know of her distress, it is exceedingly hard for him to refrain from comforting her. He wants to try to make it easy for her, from heroically and chivalrously relieving her of her burdens and taking them upon himself. If he really loves her, then he is encouraged to ask her for the opportunity to protect and care for her. The "beauty in distress" scenario is effective, but circumstances don't always justify taking advantage of this situation.

Scenario # 3: Making Action Seem Necessary, A Sudden Change of Location

There are times when a girl must leave the city or town in which she lives and choose another location. This is natural for securing action. If, through the circumstances of her life, she does not leave, the girl is sometimes justified to arrange a change of location with the sole reason of awakening the man to action.

When a man has a genuine affection for the girl, the prospects of her going where he cannot watch over her is so appalling that it will usually stir him to action. If the girl will divulge the news of her approaching departure in a romantic setting, she can make it appear that if the man is ever going to speak out, or act, now is the time. The following is an illustration of such a situation.

The Story of Mary and Robert

A girl called Mary had just graduated from college. During the last year, however, a struggling young attorney named Robert had been paying marked attention to her and had given indications of genuine affection. Knowing that he was dissatisfied with his present earnings, Mary had used the "castle in the air" method extensively in the hope of increasing his self-confidence to the point where he would not hesitate to ask her to wait for him. But Robert seemed to believe that it would be time enough to speak when his practice picked up.

He had hopes that in a year or two he could take the important step of marriage. Mary was living in the city he was in and he could speak with her about the future later as well as now. In a year from now he would be able to speak with more concrete plans and would have something worthwhile to offer her.

But Mary did not know this at all. Though she knew Robert was deeply interested in her, she was by no means sure whether he desired or ever wanted to marry her. Mary was twenty-two. She had already given him a year by letting Robert have near-monopoly of her social life. If Robert ever wanted to marry her, she wanted to know and she wanted to know it now.

Robert knew that Mary, now that she was graduated, intended to take up the teaching profession. It had not occurred to him, however, that she may teach anywhere but in their home city. Mary decided that if she prepared to leave the city to teach, Robert might be forced to speak out in order to prevent her leaving.

Now Mary could have, if she wished, taught in the schools in her home town, but she gave Robert to understand that she couldn't bear to teach under the supervision of the town's disagreeable superintendent of schools. She determined to bring matters to a head.

She waited for an opportune moment to bring up the subject. After letting slip a few meetings when either the setting was not romantic, or Robert himself was not in the right mood, she found just the situation and setting that was right for her purpose.

They spent an afternoon canoeing on the river and were gently drifting down the stream towards home. Mary softly turned the conversation to Robert, who told her for the hundredth time what his hopes and ambitions were, what victories he expected to win, what honors to achieve." Now is the time", she thought.

She told Robert she wished for some advice. She had two offers for her services as a teacher and didn't know which to take. One was from Eldorado, three hundred miles away, and the other from Mt. Pleasant, even farther. She outlined the details of the two offers. Robert, stunned at the thought, wanted to know why she couldn't teach right there at home.

She told him her reason and refused to listen to his protestations. She felt she no choice but to accept one of the two offers.

Robert was naturally aroused at this prospect of Mary's leaving him. Mary sighed and admitted she would be very lonesome, that she would feel almost in exile without him. Robert protested vigorously at her leaving the city but couldn't sway her conviction that there was no choice for her except between the two offers. She finally pouted that he was only making it harder for her to decide and begged him to help her to determine which the better offer was.

The longer he considered, the more appalling the prospect of her leaving becomes. He had always felt that Mary was sort of a fixture, that she would always be there waiting for him. He thought there was plenty of time in the future for Mary and him to reach an understanding.

What if she should go to one of these cities and meet some other man who would interest her? What if, without the guidance of her old-time friends, it should be a man who wasn't trustworthy? She shouldn't be allowed to go away alone, not if he could help it. Nobody knows little Mary like he does — her tenderness and the ease with which she could be deceived. A girl like that ought not to be allowed to go around without a man's protection.

Unaware that Robert is seething with these disturbing thoughts, Mary persisted in asking him for his opinion as to the best offer. Robert could not bring himself to tell her the one or the other. There was nothing for him to do but to tell her the truth. "You're not going to take either of those offers," he says.

"I won't stand for it. I hope to make you my wife and I want you right here where I can take care of you. I can't stand the idea of your going away on your own." Urgent necessity made him speak out.

Change of Jobs

Another example is a girl in an office who had received considerable attention from her employer, who, secretly she had fallen in love with. She came to him with an explanation that she had received a very tempting offer from another firm for her services and asked his advice regarding the acceptance of it. The man wanted to know if there was anything wrong with his treatment of her, or in the attitude of other employees towards her. Hinting that she was not free to tell him her reasons for leaving, the man was ill at ease, thinking that he had offended her in some way himself.

The girl showed a certain amount of persistence in her idea of leaving, which caused the man to find it difficult to let her go and very hard not to tell her about his desire for her to be more than an employee to him. He began to feel that the time to speak was then or never. Since he really loved the girl and was only hesitating because of an imagined obstacle, this situation made him speak out.

The Competition of Another Man

A last-resort method of awakening a man to action is to allow a complication from the attention of another man. This step is wholly justified when there seems to be no other way of encouraging a man to speak up only when you know he wants to marry you but just needs a little extra boost.

The man she really loves may consider someone else an intruder, unworthy of her. All will be unworthy of her for that matter, from his perspective. If he dislikes the other man, so much the better. He will likely have the impression that she is in danger when associating with someone other than himself. It is highly necessary for him to do something about it, but he cannot very well do anything without first explaining that he has a right to interfere because of his own feelings. Therefore, one of the easiest methods of making it appear urgent for a man to take action is to briefly date another man, especially a man who is detestable to the man you are in love with. This can strongly encourage a man to speak out before he feels prepared. Men are seldom wholly prepared for a proposal. Use this carefully. You don't really want to hurt anyone by doing this, especially the man you love.

Sexual Passion

The strongest force of emotion that will bring a man to action and cause him to take the step of marriage involves his sexual desires. Do not make the mistake of sacrificing this tool for action by indulging in sexual relations before marriage.

In other words, if a man can release these passions without marriage, he has also been relieved of his drive for marriage, or his urgency to marry. Every woman should most carefully consider this facet of moral stability. From every aspect, however, indulging in sex before marriage is foolish, and the woman is always the greatest loser.

Summary

We have given a sufficient number of examples which point out general principles involved in securing action. Any girl with a thorough understanding of these principles can adapt them to her own circumstances and her own particular man. By some method, either by those suggested here or by some other of her own devising, she must make it easier for him to act. If this is not sufficient, she must study out some way that will make it hard for him to not act, or she must place herself in such a light that action appears both urgent and necessary.

General Conclusions

We have now completed our discussions of the six stages of attracting a man. We have begun with being a girl worth having, a product of Angela Human. We have seen how attention is secured, how interest is aroused, how desire is created, how judgment is satisfied and how action is inspired.

Now, it is sometimes possible for a girl to marry a man by merely attracting his attention and interest, in rather a superficial way. This was the case with Dora in David Copperfield. But, although an adorable girl such as Dora may thus attract a man to marriage, she will not win his celestial love unless she is a girl worth having and is indispensable to his happiness.

We are not attracting men to marriage alone, but to enduring and celestial love. The steps taught here will lead you to the goal of romantic love as well as marriage. To be sure, we have had space only for the underlying principles. It remains for you to apply these principles to your own circumstances and your own society.

The mere reading of this book will not make you an expert in the art of attracting men. Many people who understand thoroughly how the orator wins his audience cannot win audiences themselves. Many people who know every aspect of salesmanship cannot sell item worth fifty cents. Many critics who are authorities on a novel cannot write one themselves. Similarly, with women, knowledge, helpful as it is, cannot take the place of practical experience. It must be put into practice. Since you will never find yourself in exactly the same circumstances as the young women in this book, you must learn to practice applying the same principles to other circumstances.

Remember too that the proper application of these principles requires a keen understanding of the characteristics of men. Every man has, in addition to common characteristics, some that are peculiar to him. To become an expert at the art of attracting men, a girl must practice the principles and skills upon as many men as possible, so that she may be familiar with the various characteristics which differ in each man.

After observing the different reactions of different men to the same situation, she will acquire a subtler and more profound understanding of the men's human nature.

Angela Human
The Ideal Woman from a Man's Point of View

Angelic Qualities

1. **Understands Men**
   a. Acceptance
   b. Admiration
   c. Sensitive Pride
   d. Sympathetic-Understanding
   e. Desire for superiority in his role
   f. Make him No. 1
2. **Has Deep Inner Happiness**
   a. A result of character
   b. Result of domestic goodness
   c. Accept ourselves
   d. Ability to appreciate appreciate life
3. **Has a Lovely Character**
   a. Self Mastery
   b. Unselfishness
   c. Benevolence
   d. Moral Courage
   e. Patience
   f. Chastity
   g. Honesty
   h. Humility
   i. Self Dignity
   j. Gentle Tender Qualtiy
4. **Is a Domestic Goddess**
   a. Good homemaker
   b. Good mother
   c. Happy in role

Human Qualities

1. **Femininity**
   a. In Appearance
   b. In Manner
   c. Feminine dependency in actions and attitude towards men
2. **Radiates Happiness**
   a. Cheerful
   b. Sheds joy around
   c. Presence lights the home
3. **Fresh Appearance and Manner**
   a. Has good health
   b. Appears fresh in
      1. Cleanliness
      2. Grooming
      3. Dress
4. **Child-like-ness**
   a. Child-like Emotions
      1. Unhappy Emotions
      2. Tender Emotion
      3. Changeful Emotions
      4. Joy
   b. Asking for things
   c. Child-like manner
   d. Child-like dress

Together He Cherishes. Both Are Essential to His Celestial Love.

The Angelic arouses in man a feeling approaching worship. It brings him peace and happiness. The Human fascinates, captivates, amuses, enchants and arouses a desire to protect and shelter.

The 6 Stages of Winning a Man

FIRST STAGE: Be a girl Worth Having.

How: Acquire all of the qualities of Angela Human.

SECOND STAGE: Win his attention.

How:

  1. By a feminine and girlish appearance.

  2. By a feminine manner.

  3. By feminine need of him.

THIRD STAGE: Arousing Attention.

How:

  1. Get him to confide.

  2. Admire the manly.

FOURTH STAGE: Creating Desire.

How:

1. Prove you are a girl worth having (by being Angela Human).

2. Become indispensable to his happiness (applying all of Understanding Men).

FIFTH STAGE: Overcome Judgment (Removing Obstacles).

How:

1. By building castles in the air.

2. Other miscellaneous methods.

SIXTH STAGE: Securing Action.

How:

1. Making it easy for him to act.

2. Making it hard not to act.

3. Making action appear urgent or necessary.

Remember to "aim high" — aim to be Angela Human. Don't be content to sit on the sidelines and let all of the other girls succeed in attracting desirable men. You can just as well be enjoying the "flowers of life" rather than the "weeds." You can "eat the banquet" instead of the "crumbs which fall beneath the table." Through study and effort you can become a fascinating woman, as fascinating and sought after by men as any of God's other womanly creatures.

Life is a piece of paper, white
On which each one of us must write
his word or two, and then comes night.
Greatly begin, though thou hast time
but for a line, be that sublime
Not failure, but low aim is crime.

~ James Russell Lowell.

Angelic and Human Don'ts

❖ Don't try to change a man.

❖ Don't offer suggestions, hints, etc., about how he needs to improve.

❖ Don't use other men as perfect examples.

❖ Don't show indifference, contempt or ridicule towards his masculine abilities, achievements or ideas.

❖ Don't try to solve his problems but give him the courage to do so.

❖ Don't try to excel him in anything which requires masculine strength, skill or ability.

❖ Don't tell men what to do or where to go or give pushy advice or suggestions.

❖ Don't plan a career for yourself which could damage your success as a wonderful wife, mother and homemaker.

❖ Avoid concentrating on material things as a means to happiness.

- Don't criticize yourself for common mistakes and human errors.
- Don't fall from your pedestal by lowering your standards or by being harsh or critical, etc.
- Don't appear to be too eager.
- Don't man hunt.
- Don't wear masculine styles, materials, accessories.
- Don't act, look or talk like men.
- Don't use harsh, crude or vulgar words or actions.
- Don't be loud or boisterous.
- Don't disregard another person's culture.
- Don't be aggressive or dominating.
- Don't be too capable, efficient, or competent in masculine jobs.
- Don't boss men around, tell them what to do, where to go, etc.
- Don't be competitive with men in their own fields if you want to attract one.
- Don't deliberately excel men in anything which requires masculine strength, skill or ability.
- Don't be gloomy or overly serious.
- Don't wear drab or masculine clothing.
- Don't bury wounded feelings.

❖ Don't let men impose on you, treat you unfairly, ignore you or insult you too far.

❖ Don't suppress the tendency to cry in sad movies or situations, or when your feelings are hurt.

❖ Don't wear matronly styles.

❖ Don't be evasive or make endless explanations to men.

❖ If you want something, don't, hint, attempt to convince, or demand.

❖ Don't sit at home where men cannot find you.

❖ Do not indulge in too much physical affection during the early stages of romance.

❖ Don't show your feeling of love to him before you are certain he returns your feelings.

❖ Don't be aggressive in romance, don't try to kiss him before he is ready, take his hand, squeeze close to him, ask him for a date, ask to marry him.

❖ Don't indulge in sexual relations before marriage.

❖ Don't be impatient if a man is slow to make up his mind about you.

Angelic and Human Do's

❖ Accept him at face value.

❖ Allow him to be himself.

❖ Admire the manly things about him.

- Understand his masculine responsibilities and his drive for status.
- Recognize his superior strength and ability in masculine things.
- Need his masculine care and protection.
- Respect the man's position as a leader; be a good follower. This is limited before marriage.
- Have a girlish trust in him, in his ability to solve problems and meet emergencies.
- Accept yourself and allow for many mistakes.
- Enjoy the simple pleasures in life.
- Develop a character worthy of a pedestal.
- Learn to be a Domestic Goddess.
- Enjoy homemaking (even if it's just your room or dorm room).
- Do it well.
- Add feminine touches.
- Be well organized.
- Learn to handle money wisely.
- Let good homemaking become second nature to you.
- Wear feminine clothes, styles and materials which make you look feminine.
- Wear clothes that are modest.

❖ Accentuate the differences between yourself and men in your appearance, manner and actions.

❖ Be refined, tactful, diplomatic, considerate, polite and socially well bred.

❖ Need a man's care and protection.

❖ If you are "stuck" with a masculine job, do it in a feminine manner.

❖ Allow yourself to need men for their care and protection.

❖ Yield to the man's suggestions (except with your own standards and ideals — in these be firm and do not yield) This is limited when you aren't married to him.

❖ Radiate happiness and shed joy around.

❖ Strive for abundant health.

❖ Maintain your weight for health and self-esteem.

❖ When men are thoughtless and unkind, respond with sauciness.

❖ When a man is stern, cross, or overly serious, respond with teasing playfulness.

❖ When a man gives you a gift or does something nice for you, respond with childlike joy.

❖ Let men spoil you and do things for you.

❖ Be direct and outspoken (not blunt).

❖ If you want something, "ask for it" in a girlish manner. This is also limited before marriage.

- ❖ Work on self-esteem.

- ❖ Learn to be a good conversationalist.

- ❖ As often as possible attend social affairs where men are present.

- ❖ Practice being a good hostess.

- ❖ Encourage a large circle of friends — girls, boys, old people and children.

- ❖ In choosing a mate, look for traits of character, masculinity, and kindness.

- ❖ Avoid abusive men of low character or who are alcoholics, drug abusers or criminals.

- ❖ Let the man lead in romance and you follow.(There are exceptions once in awhile).

- ❖ Keep him guessing where appropriate.

- ❖ If a man is slow to make up his mind about you, create romantic situations.

- ❖ If a man will not make up is mind about you, even after great patience, bring him to action by the methods taught.

Success Stories

#1

"My girlfriend's daughter changed overnight after reading The Fascinating Girl. Her sarcasm and impatience disappeared as she began to understand her own role in life and to have more confidence in herself as she put into practice F.G. I wish the book was used in high school and home economics classes."

#2

"At age 26 I resigned myself to being an old maid, never having a family of my own or finding a mate to share life with. Both of these last two goals seem to come so easily to other women. I began to be puzzled and bitter and tortured with a complex because it looked as if I just couldn't measure up to other women by landing a husband. Everyone told me how pretty I was, how well dressed, how competent in my career and yet I could not manage to keep a man interested in me very long.

As a result, I often sank into states of depression, wore a sour look on my face and gradually developed into the stereotyped image of an "old maid"—crotchety and self-righteous.

One night while watching T.V., I saw Mrs. Andelin and Beulah Hodge in the middle of an interview. They were discussing Fascinating Womanhood. After that I went out and bought a copy and how glad I am that I did. Reading it made me realize it was my own fault I wasn't sought after by men. I had put too much emphasis on outer appearance and not enough on inner charm. It was I and not the men of this world who had to change.

Putting this task before me, I set out to change my sour expression to one of joy, my independent manner to one of feminine dependency, my unbending will of iron to one of yielding and my selfish, self-centeredness to an attitude of concern for the feelings of others.

On dates with men I had been firm in my opinions, critical of other people and just plain thoughtless. No wonder I "turned off" men. Nothing is more repulsive to them than a forthright female with hard opinions and an aggressive manner. I read and reread The Fascinating Girl, underlining in ink the important points I had to work on. Gradually the precepts of the book began to soak into my mind.

As luck would have it, I scanned the hobby paper and answered an ad wanting movie material, quoting source I knew of. A week later a note of thanks came from the advertiser. One thing led to another and soon he and I were corresponding regularly. From this man's letters I could sense he was a lonely person with little self-confidence. He was consistently making belittling remarks about himself and his looks. I saw in him a chance to practice the precepts of Fascinating Girl and at the same time help to comfort another human being. I had no idea it would lead to marriage.

My heart went out to this *Ma* because I knew too well how awful loneliness can be. In each letter I took every opportunity to admire him, to encourage him to talk about himself and his interests and build up his badly deflated ego. He was thirty-four years old, a bachelor living at home and very much in need o a little old-fashioned admiration from a woman. His pride was nil. He had given up on all women and had withdrawn into a silent shell, living only for his hobby and leading a dull kind of life.

Chapter 25: The Proposal

Ever so slowly he let down his reserve and told me he looked forward to getting a letter from me. "You are the only woman who has ever appreciated me", he wrote. All along the crying need of his soul had been the attention and admiration of a woman. Years of self-depreciation melted away as I continued to make him feel my sincere regard for his many fine qualities.

For example, whenever he described himself as a "120 pound weakling" I countered with a favorable comment on his physique. When he said he was clumsy and awkward I wrote back that I found that impossible to believe from his letters and pictures. Being a sensitive person, he felt badly due to his lack of a high school diploma. While he was a teenager his mother became mentally ill and he had to quit school in the 9th grade to stay home and take care of his small brothers and sisters. His father had died earlier.

When he revealed this to me, I chose to praise him for making such a noble sacrifice for his family. Each time he cut himself down; I tried to comfort his wounded pride.

Last month we met in person for the first time and hit it off very well. I continued to admire him in every way I could think of and before my eyes, he changed from a timid, ill-at-ease man into a confident male. Basking in the sun of a woman's sincere appreciation was all he ever needed to make him feel equal to other men. Tears of love filled his eyes as he looked at me and declared "You are the most wonderful thing that has happened to me!"

Unexpectedly I found myself worshiped, courted and adored beyond my wildest daydreams. He turned out to be endlessly thoughtful and protective and romantic. Since then, he hasn't stopped telling me how much he loves me. I hardly recognize the man I started writing to many months before.

Fascinating Girl works! I am sure because next month we will be married and start a life of our own. Both our lives are changed.

Any woman who moves out into a man's world to conquer it and compete with him is a fool. Not only is she a fool but she is unknowingly destroying the chances of finding the very thing she is secretly looking for—the same thing every woman has wanted since Eve—the love of a man. This philosophy is not a bag of tricks but a new way of life. The day I bought a copy of The Fascinating Girl was the luckiest day of my life.

About the Author

Helen Andelin had eight children and a happy marriage by the time she began teaching marriage enrichment classes in her late 30s. She would devote the rest of her long life to helping women get the most out of their lives and relationships. Fascinating Womanhood went on to become an international best seller. Together with other books that she wrote afterwards, Helen Andelin's work spawned a global movement that has helped hundreds of thousands of relationships around the world.

Helen Berry Andelin was born in Mesa, Arizona in 1920 to May and Herbert Berry, a dentist. Raised in a happy home where education was emphasized, Helen attended college to study home economics. "Even though times were hard, working in a malt shop for ten cents per hour, sewing curtains and ironing sheets for my parents' motel, the depression was a time when people worked together and appreciated simple things," states the author.

Helen began her loving marriage to Aubrey Andelin in 1942. They first lived in Los Angeles where Aubrey attended dental school at the University of Southern California, and later served in the Air Force. While raising four sons and four daughters, and teaching marriage classes, Helen began writing Fascinating Womanhood. Her classes became *standing room only*. Her first version of Fascinating Womanhood was printed by a local high school yearbook company in 1963. In 1974, after selling more than 400,000 copies out of her garage, and with 700 certified teachers, Helen signed a contract with a major New York publisher. To date, her book has sold about 5 million copies worldwide.

Helen passed away in 2009, leaving her work and the movement to her daughters, and charging the eldest, Dixie Andelin Forsyth, with the task of updating Fascinating Womanhood, and also writing a sequel entitled Fascinating Womanhood For the Timeless Woman.

About the Editor

Dixie Andelin Forsyth is the eldest of Helen Andelin's four daughters, and one of her mother's protégées during the height of the Fascinating Womanhood movement. It was Helen Andelin's intention to write a follow-up book to Fascinating Womanhood: an update to reflect changes in modern culture. Before she passed away, Helen asked Dixie to take up this task. She was raised with the teachings of Fascinating Womanhood under the guidance and personal tutelage of the author from an early age.

In her private life, she is happily married and the mother of seven children, an accomplished artist, and homemaker. Dixie is the author of the sequel Fascinating Womanhood For the Timeless Woman, scheduled to be printed in 2017.

Dixie is the current President of Fascinating Womanhood. Fascinating Womanhood can be found on the web at FascinatingWomanhood.com, and on Facebook at @TheRealFascinatingWomanhood.

Made in United States
North Haven, CT
02 April 2023

34835612R00186